Real Estate Accounting

A Practitioner's Guide

Third Edition

Steven M. Bragg

For more information about AccountingTools® products, visit our Web site at www.accountingtools.com.

ISBN-13: 978-1-64221-034-7

Printed in the United States of America

Table of Contents

Preface

There are many kinds of real estate transactions, each of which must be accounted for in its own unique way. These events include the sale of time-share intervals, the purchase of income-producing property, the construction of a new facility using debt financing, property swaps, and the sale of land. *Real Estate Accounting* shows how to properly account for each of these transactions and many more, as well as how to disclose them in one's financial statements.

The book is divided into two sections. In Chapters 1 through 6, we focus on the main real estate activities of building or buying property, followed by its sale to a third party. In Chapters 7 through 11, we deal with more specialized topics. These topics include time-sharing activities, rental transactions, asset retirement obligations, real estate ventures, and housing associations.

You can find the answers to many questions about real estate accounting in the following chapters, including:

- Which preacquisition costs can I capitalize?
- How do I capitalize the cost of interest into a real estate project?
- Do I recognize goodwill when buying an income-producing property?
- What are the criteria for using the different income recognition methods?
- How do I account for an exchange of property?
- How do I account for the sale of a time-share interval?
- What types of leases can be offered to a prospective tenant?
- How do I account for asset retirement obligations?
- How does an investor account for an interest in a real estate venture?

Real Estate Accounting is designed primarily for professionals, who can use it as a reference tool for determining the most appropriate accounting treatment of different real estate transactions.

Centennial, Colorado
November 2019

About the Author

Steven Bragg, CPA, has been the chief financial officer or controller of four companies, as well as a consulting manager at Ernst & Young. He received a master's degree in finance from Bentley College, an MBA from Babson College, and a Bachelor's degree in Economics from the University of Maine. He has been a two-time president of the Colorado Mountain Club, and is an avid alpine skier, mountain biker, and certified master diver. Mr. Bragg resides in Centennial, Colorado. He has written the following books and courses:

7 Habits of Effective CEOs	Change Management
7 Habits of Effective CFOs	Closing the Books
7 Habits of Effective Controllers	Coaching and Mentoring
Accountant Ethics [for multiple states]	Conflict Management
Accountants' Guidebook	Constraint Management
Accounting Changes and Error Corrections	Construction Accounting
Accounting Controls Guidebook	Corporate Bankruptcy
Accounting for Breweries	Corporate Cash Management
Accounting for Casinos and Gaming	Corporate Finance
Accounting for Derivatives and Hedges	Cost Accounting (college textbook)
Accounting for Earnings per Share	Cost Accounting Fundamentals
Accounting for Income Taxes	Cost Management Guidebook
Accounting for Intangible Assets	CPA Firm Mergers and Acquisitions
Accounting for Inventory	Credit & Collection Guidebook
Accounting for Investments	Crowdfunding
Accounting for Leases	Developing and Managing Teams
Accounting for Managers	Effective Collections
Accounting for Mining	Effective Employee Training
Accounting for Retirement Benefits	Effective Innovation
Accounting for Stock-Based Compensation	Effective Negotiation
Accounting for Vineyards and Wineries	Effective Time Management
Accounting Information Systems	Employee Onboarding
Accounting Procedures Guidebook	Enterprise Risk Management
Activity-Based Costing	Entertainment Industry Accounting
Activity-Based Management	Ethical Frameworks in Accounting
Agricultural Accounting	Ethical Responsibilities
Auditor Independence	Excel Charts and Visualizations
Behavioral Ethics	Excel Data Analysis Tools
Bookkeeping Guidebook	Excel Data Management
Budgeting	Excel Formulas and Functions
Business Combinations and Consolidations	Fair Value Accounting
Business Insurance Fundamentals	Fiduciary Accounting
Business Ratios	Financial Analysis
Business Strategy	Financial Forecasting and Modeling
Business Valuation	Fixed Asset Accounting
Capital Budgeting	Foreign Currency Accounting
CFO Guidebook	Franchise Accounting

On-Line Resources by Steven Bragg

Steven maintains the accountingtools.com web site, which contains continuing professional education courses, the Accounting Best Practices podcast, and thousands of articles on accounting subjects.

Real Estate Accounting is also available as a continuing professional education (CPE) course. You can purchase the course (and many other courses) and take an on-line exam at: **www.accountingtools.com/cpe**

Chapter 1
Introduction to Accounting

Introduction

Before one can engage in real estate accounting activities, it is first necessary to understand the basic underpinnings of accounting, as well as the general flow of accounting transactions. In this chapter, we describe the essentials of financial accounting, which includes how accounting transactions are recorded using journal entries. We also address the types of business entities that can be used to engage in real estate activities, along with the advantages and disadvantages of each one. This information is useful for understanding the details of real estate accounting, as presented in the following chapters.

Financial Accounting Basics

This introductory section is intended to give an overview of financial accounting basics. Its orientation is toward recording financial information about a business.

First, what do we mean by "financial" accounting? This refers to the recordation of information about money. Thus, we will talk about issuing an invoice to someone, as well as their payment of that invoice, but we will not address any change in the value of a company's overall business, since the latter situation does not involve a specific transaction involving money.

A *transaction* is a business event that has a monetary impact, such as selling goods to a customer or buying supplies from a vendor. In financial accounting, a transaction triggers the recording of information about the money involved in the event. For example, we would record in the accounting records such events (transactions) as:

- Incurring debt from a lender
- The receipt of an expense report from an employee
- Selling property to a buyer
- Paying sales taxes to the government
- Paying wages to employees

We record this information in *accounts*. An account is a separate, detailed record about a specific item, such as expenditures for office supplies, or accounts receivable, or accounts payable. There can be many accounts, of which the most common are:

- *Cash.* This is the current balance of cash held by a business, usually in checking or savings accounts.
- *Accounts receivable.* These are sales on credit, which customers must pay for at a later date.
- *Inventory.* This is items held in stock, for eventual sale to customers.

- *Fixed assets.* These are more expensive assets that the business plans to use for multiple years.
- *Accounts payable.* These are liabilities payable to suppliers that have not yet been paid.
- *Accrued expenses.* These are liabilities for which the business has not yet been billed, but for which it will eventually have to pay.
- *Debt.* This is cash loaned to the business by another party.
- *Equity.* This is the ownership interest in the business, which is the founding capital and any subsequent profits that have been retained in the business.
- *Revenue.* This is sales made to buyers.
- *Cost of goods sold.* This is the cost of goods or services sold to customers. It could include the cost of properties sold.
- *Administrative expenses.* These are a variety of expenses required to run a business, such as salaries, rent, utilities, and office supplies.
- *Income taxes.* These are the taxes paid to the government on any income earned by the business.

How do we enter information about transactions into these accounts? There are two ways to do so:

- *Software module entries.* If accounting software is used to record financial accounting transactions, there will probably be on-line forms to fill out for each of the major transactions, such as creating an invoice or recording a supplier invoice. Every time one of these forms is filled out, the software automatically populates the accounts for the user.
- *Journal entries.* One can access a journal entry form in the accounting software, or create a journal entry by hand. This is a more customized way to record accounting information.

The accounts are stored in the *general ledger.* This is the master set of all accounts, in which are stored all of the business transactions that have been entered into the accounts with journal entries or software module entries. There may be subsidiary ledgers in which are stored high-volume transactions, such as sales or purchases. Thus, the general ledger is the go-to document for all of the detailed financial accounting information about a business.

To understand the detail for a particular account, such as the current amount of accounts receivable outstanding, access the general ledger for this information. In addition, most accounting software packages provide a number of reports that give better insights into the business than just reading through the accounts. In particular, there are aged accounts receivable and aged accounts payable reports that are useful for determining the current list of uncollected accounts receivable and unpaid accounts payable, respectively.

The general ledger is also the source document for the financial statements. There are several financial statements, which are:

- *Balance sheet.* This report lists the assets, liabilities, and equity of the business as of the report date.
- *Income statement.* This report lists the revenues, expenses, and profit or loss of the business for a specific period of time.
- *Statement of cash flows.* This report lists the cash inflows and outflows generated by the business for a specific period of time.

In summary, we have shown that financial accounting involves the recording of business transactions in accounts, which in turn are summarized in the general ledger, which in turn is used to create financial statements. We will now walk through the building blocks of an accounting system, starting with the accounting frameworks from which accounting rules are derived.

Accounting Frameworks

The accounting profession operates under a set of guidelines for how business transactions are to be recorded and reported. There are a multitude of transactions that an organization might enter into, so the corresponding guidelines are also quite large. These guidelines can be subject to a considerable amount of interpretation, so there are standard-setting bodies that maintain and support the guidelines with official pronouncements.

Not every organization operates under the same set of guidelines. There may be different guidelines for different types of entities, and slight differences in guidelines by country. Each of these unique guidelines is referred to as an accounting framework. Once an organization adopts a certain accounting framework, it continues to record transactions and report financial results in accordance with the rules of that framework on a long-term basis. Doing so provides the users of its financial reports with a considerable amount of reporting continuity. Also, because an accounting framework provides a consistent set of rules, anyone reading the financial statements of multiple companies that employ the same framework has a reasonable basis for comparison.

The most commonly-used accounting framework in the United States is GAAP, which is short for Generally Accepted Accounting Principles. GAAP is the most comprehensive accounting framework in the world, with an extensive set of detailed rules covering a massive range of accounting topics. GAAP also provides rules for how to handle accounting transactions in specific industries, such as mining, airlines, health care, and – of course – real estate.

GAAP is derived from the pronouncements of a series of government-sponsored accounting entities, of which the Financial Accounting Standards Board is the latest. The Securities and Exchange Commission also issues accounting pronouncements through its Staff Accounting Bulletins and other announcements that are applicable only to publicly-held companies, and which are considered to be part of GAAP.

International Financial Reporting Standards, or IFRS, is the accounting framework used in most other countries. GAAP is much more rules-based than IFRS, which focuses more on general principles than GAAP. This focus makes the IFRS body of work much smaller, cleaner, and easier to understand than GAAP.

There are several working groups that are gradually reducing the differences between the GAAP and IFRS accounting frameworks, so eventually there should be minor differences in the reported results of a business if it switches between the two frameworks.

The accounting information in this book is based on the GAAP framework. At the higher level of discussion used in this book, there are few notable differences between GAAP and IFRS.

The Accounting Cycle

The accounting cycle is a sequential set of activities used to identify and record an entity's individual transactions. These transactions are then aggregated at the end of each reporting period into financial statements. The accounting cycle is essentially the core recordation activity that an accountant engages in, and is the basis upon which the financial statements are constructed. The following discussion breaks the accounting cycle into the treatment of individual transactions and then closing the books at the end of the accounting period. The accounting cycle for individual transactions is:

1. Identify the event causing an accounting transaction, such as buying materials, paying wages to employees, or selling property to buyers.
2. Prepare the business document associated with the accounting transaction, such as a supplier invoice, buyer invoice, or cash receipt.
3. Identify which accounts are affected by the business document.
4. Record in the appropriate accounts in the accounting database the amounts noted on the business document.

The preceding accounting cycle steps were associated with individual transactions. The following accounting cycle steps are only used at the end of the reporting period, and are associated with the aggregate amounts of the preceding transactions:

5. Prepare a preliminary trial balance, which itemizes the debit and credit totals for each account.
6. Add accrued items, record estimated reserves, and correct errors in the preliminary trial balance with adjusting entries. Examples are the recordation of an expense for supplier invoices that have not yet arrived, and accruing for unpaid wages earned.
7. Prepare an adjusted trial balance, which incorporates the preliminary trial balance and all adjusting entries. It may require several iterations before this report accurately reflects the results of operations of the business.
8. Prepare financial statements from the adjusted trial balance.
9. Close the books for the reporting period.

In the following sections, we expand upon a number of the concepts just noted in the accounting cycle, including accounting transactions and journal entries.

Accounting Transactions

An accounting transaction is a business event having a monetary impact on the financial statements of a business. It is recorded in the accounting records of an organization. Examples of accounting transactions are:

- Sale in cash to a buyer
- Sale on credit to a buyer
- Receive cash in payment of an invoice owed by a buyer
- Purchase fixed assets from a supplier
- Record the depreciation of a fixed asset over time
- Purchase consumable supplies from a supplier
- Investment in another business
- Borrow funds from a lender
- Issue a dividend to investors
- Sale of assets to a third party

Types of Transaction Cycles

A transaction cycle is an interlocking set of business transactions. Most business transactions can be aggregated into a relatively small number of transaction cycles related to the sale of goods or property, payments to suppliers, payments to employees, and payments to lenders. We explore the nature of these transaction cycles in the following bullet points:

- *Sales cycle*. A company sells property to a buyer, issues an invoice, and collects payment. This set of sequential, interrelated activities is known as the sales cycle, or revenue cycle.
- *Purchasing cycle*. A company issues a purchase order to a supplier for goods, receives the goods, records an account payable, and pays the supplier. There are several ancillary activities, such as the use of petty cash or procurement cards for smaller purchases. This set of sequential, interrelated activities is known as the purchasing cycle, or expenditure cycle.
- *Payroll cycle*. A company records the time of its employees, verifies hours and overtime worked, calculates gross pay, deducts taxes and other withholdings, and issues paychecks to employees. Other related activities include the payment of withheld income taxes to the government, as well as the issuance of annual W-2 forms to employees. This cluster of activities is known as the payroll cycle.
- *Financing cycle*. A company borrows money from lenders, followed by a series of interest payments and repayments of the debt. Also, a company issues stock to investors, in exchange for periodic dividend payments and other payouts if the entity is dissolved. These clusters of transactions are more diverse than the preceding transaction cycles, but may involve substantially more money.

A key role of the accountant is to design an appropriate set of procedures, forms, and integrated controls for each of these transaction cycles, to mitigate the opportunities for fraud and ensure that transactions are processed in as reliable and consistent a manner as possible.

Source Documents

Source documents are the physical basis upon which business transactions are recorded. They usually contain the following information:

- A description of the transaction
- The date of the transaction
- A specific amount of money
- An authorizing signature (in some cases)

Examples of source documents and their related business transactions that appear in the financial records are:

- *Bank statement.* This contains a number of adjustments to a company's book balance of cash on hand that the company should reference to bring its records into alignment with those of a bank.
- *Credit card receipt.* This can be used as evidence for a disbursement of funds from petty cash.
- *Lockbox check images.* These images support the recordation of cash receipts from customers.
- *Supplier invoice.* This document supports the issuance of a cash, check, or electronic payment to a supplier. A supplier invoice also supports the recordation of an expense, inventory item, or fixed asset.
- *Time card.* This supports the issuance of a paycheck or electronic payment to an employee. If employee hours are being billed to customers, the time card also supports the creation of customer invoices.

Double Entry Accounting

Double entry accounting is a record keeping system under which every transaction is recorded in at least two accounts. There is no upper limit on the number of accounts used in a transaction, but the minimum is two accounts. There are two columns in each account, with debit entries on the left and credit entries on the right. In double entry accounting, the total of all debit entries must match the total of all credit entries. When this happens, a transaction is said to be *in balance*. If the totals do not agree, the transaction is *out of balance*. An out of balance transaction must be corrected before financial statements can be created.

The definitions of a debit and credit are:

- A debit is an accounting entry that either increases an asset or expense account, or decreases a liability or equity account. It is positioned to the left in an accounting entry.
- A credit is an accounting entry that either increases a liability or equity account, or decreases an asset or expense account. It is positioned to the right in an accounting entry.

An account is a separate, detailed record associated with a specific asset, liability, equity, revenue, expense, gain, or loss. Examples of accounts are noted in the following table.

Characteristics of Sample Accounts

Account Name	Account Type	Normal Account Balance
Cash	Asset	Debit
Accounts receivable	Asset	Debit
Inventory	Asset	Debit
Fixed assets	Asset	Debit
Accounts payable	Liability	Credit
Accrued liabilities	Liability	Credit
Notes payable	Liability	Credit
Common stock	Equity	Credit
Retained earnings	Equity	Credit
Revenue - products	Revenue	Credit
Revenue - services	Revenue	Credit
Cost of goods sold	Expense	Debit
Compensation expense	Expense	Debit
Utilities expense	Expense	Debit
Travel and entertainment	Expense	Debit
Gain on sale of asset	Gain	Credit
Loss on sale of asset	Loss	Debit

The key point with double entry accounting is that a single transaction always triggers a recordation in *at least* two accounts, as assets and liabilities gradually flow through a business and are converted into revenues, expenses, gains, and losses. We expand upon this concept in the next section.

The Accounting Equation

The accounting equation is the basis upon which the double entry accounting system is constructed. In essence, the accounting equation is:

$$\text{Assets} = \text{Liabilities} + \text{Shareholders' Equity}$$

The assets in the accounting equation are the resources that a company has available for its use, such as cash, accounts receivable, fixed assets, and inventory. The company pays for these resources by either incurring liabilities (which is the Liabilities part of the accounting equation) or by obtaining funding from investors (which is the Shareholders' Equity part of the equation). Thus, there are resources with offsetting claims against those resources, either from creditors or investors.

The Liabilities part of the equation is usually comprised of accounts payable that are owed to suppliers, a variety of accrued liabilities, such as sales taxes and income taxes, and debt payable to lenders.

The Shareholders' Equity part of the equation is more complex than simply being the amount paid to the company by investors. It is actually their initial investment, plus any subsequent gains, minus any subsequent losses, minus any dividends or other withdrawals paid to the investors.

This relationship between assets, liabilities, and shareholders' equity appears in the balance sheet, where the total of all assets always equals the sum of the liabilities and shareholders' equity sections.

The reason why the accounting equation is so important is that it is always true - and it forms the basis for all accounting transactions. At a general level, this means that whenever there is a recordable transaction, the choices for recording it all involve keeping the accounting equation in balance.

EXAMPLE

Creekside Industrial engages in the following series of transactions:

1. Creekside sells shares to an investor for $10,000. This increases the cash (asset) account as well as the capital (equity) account.
2. Creekside buys $4,000 of building materials from a supplier. This increases the inventory (asset) account as well as the payables (liability) account.
3. Creekside sells the inventory for $6,000. This decreases the inventory (asset) account and creates a cost of goods sold expense that appears as a decrease in the income (equity) account.
4. The sale of Creekside's inventory also creates a sale and offsetting receivable. This increases the receivables (asset) account by $6,000 and increases the income (equity) account by $6,000.
5. Creekside collects cash from the customer to which it sold the inventory. This increases the cash (asset) account by $6,000 and decreases the receivables (asset) account by $6,000.

These transactions appear in the following table:

Item	(Asset) Cash	(Asset) Receivables	(Asset) Inventory		(Liability) Payables	(Equity) Capital	(Equity) Income
(1)	$10,000			=		$10,000	
(2)			$4,000	=	$4,000		
(3)			-4,000	=			-$4,000
(4)		$6,000		=			6,000
(5)	6,000	-6,000		=			
Totals	$16,000	$0	$0	=	$4,000	$10,000	$2,000

In the example, note how every transaction is balanced within the accounting equation - either because there are changes on both sides of the equation, or because a transaction cancels itself out on one side of the equation (as was the case when the receivable was converted to cash).

The following table shows how a number of typical accounting transactions are recorded within the framework of the accounting equation.

Accounting Equation Examples

Transaction Type	Assets	Liabilities + Equity
Buy fixed assets on credit	Fixed assets increase	Accounts payable (liability) increases
Buy inventory on credit	Inventory increases	Accounts payable (liability) increases
Pay dividends	Cash decreases	Retained earnings (equity) decreases
Pay rent	Cash decreases	Income (equity) decreases
Pay supplier invoices	Cash decreases	Accounts payable (liability) decreases
Sell property on credit (part 1)	Inventory decreases	Income (equity) decreases
Sell property on credit (part 2)	Accounts receivable increases	Income (equity) increases
Sell stock	Cash increases	Equity increases

Here are examples of each of the preceding transactions, where we show how they comply with the accounting equation:

- *Buy fixed assets on credit*. Creekside buys a machine on credit for $10,000. This increases the fixed assets (asset) account and increases the accounts payable (liability) account. Thus, the asset and liability sides of the transaction are equal.
- *Buy inventory on credit*. Creekside buys materials on credit for $5,000. This increases the inventory (asset) account and increases the accounts payable (liability) account. Thus, the asset and liability sides of the transaction are equal.
- *Pay dividends*. Creekside pays $25,000 in dividends. This reduces the cash (asset) account and reduces the retained earnings (equity) account. Thus, the asset and equity sides of the transaction are equal.

9

- *Pay rent.* Creekside pays $4,000 in rent. This reduces the cash (asset) account and reduces the accounts payable (liabilities) account. Thus, the asset and liability sides of the transaction are equal.
- *Pay supplier invoices.* Creekside pays $29,000 on existing supplier invoices. This reduces the cash (asset) account by $29,000 and reduces the accounts payable (liability) account. Thus, the asset and liability sides of the transaction are equal.
- *Sell property on credit.* Creekside sells property for $55,000 on credit. This increases the accounts receivable (asset) account by $55,000, and increases the revenue (equity) account. Thus, the asset and equity sides of the transaction are equal.
- *Sell stock.* Creekside sells $120,000 of its shares to investors. This increases the cash account (asset) by $120,000, and increases the capital stock (equity) account. Thus, the asset and equity sides of the transaction are equal.

Journal Entries

A journal entry is a formalized method for recording a business transaction. It is recorded in the accounting records of a business, usually in the general ledger, but sometimes in a subsidiary ledger that is then summarized and rolled forward into the general ledger.

Journal entries are used in a double entry accounting system, where the intent is to record every business transaction in at least two places. For example, when a company sells property for cash, this increases both the revenue account and the cash account. Or, if materials are acquired on account, this increases both the accounts payable account and the inventory account.

The structure of a journal entry is:

- A header line may include a journal entry number and entry date.
- The first column includes the account number and account name into which the entry is recorded. This field is indented if it is for the account being credited.
- The second column contains the debit amount to be entered.
- The third column contains the credit amount to be entered.
- A footer line may also include a brief description of the reason for the entry.

Thus, the basic journal entry format is:

	Debit	Credit
Account name / number	$xx,xxx	
Account name / number		$xx,xxx

The structural rules of a journal entry are that there must be a minimum of two line items in the entry, and that the total amount entered in the debit column equals the total amount entered in the credit column.

A journal entry is usually printed and stored in a binder of accounting transactions, with backup materials attached that justify the entry. This information may be accessed by the company's auditors as part of their annual audit activities.

There are several types of journal entries, including:

- *Adjusting entry*. An adjusting entry is used at month-end to alter the financial statements to bring them into compliance with the relevant accounting framework. For example, a company could accrue unpaid wages at month-end in order to recognize the wages expense in the current period.
- *Compound entry*. This is a journal entry that includes more than two lines of entries. It is frequently used to record complex transactions, or several transactions at once. For example, the journal entry to record a payroll usually contains many lines, since it involves the recordation of numerous tax liabilities and payroll deductions.
- *Reversing entry*. This is an adjusting entry that is reversed as of the beginning of the following period, usually because an expense was accrued in the preceding period, and is no longer needed. Thus, a wage accrual in the preceding period is reversed in the next period, to be replaced by an actual payroll expenditure.

In general, journal entries are not used to record high-volume transactions, such as supplier invoices. These transactions are handled through specialized software modules that present a standard on-line form to be filled out. Once the form is complete, the software automatically creates the accounting record.

The Ledger Concept

A *ledger* is a book or database in which double-entry accounting transactions are stored or summarized. A *subsidiary ledger* is a ledger designed for the storage of specific types of accounting transactions. If a subsidiary ledger is used, the information in it is then summarized and posted to an account in the *general ledger*, which in turn is used to construct the financial statements of a company. The account in the general ledger where this summarized information is stored is called a *control account*. Most accounts in the general ledger are not control accounts; instead, transactions are recorded directly into them.

A subsidiary ledger can be set up to offload data storage for virtually any general ledger account. However, they are usually only created for areas in which there are high transaction volumes, which limits their use to a few areas. Examples of subsidiary ledgers are:

- Accounts receivable ledger
- Fixed assets ledger

- Inventory ledger
- Purchases ledger

> **Tip:** Subsidiary ledgers are used when there is a large amount of transaction information that would clutter up the general ledger. This situation typically arises in companies with significant sales volume. Thus, there may be no need for subsidiary ledgers in a small company.

The following chart shows how the various data entry modules within an accounting system are used to create transactions which are recorded in either the general ledger or various subsidiary ledgers, and which are eventually aggregated to create the financial statements.

Transaction Flow in the Accounting System

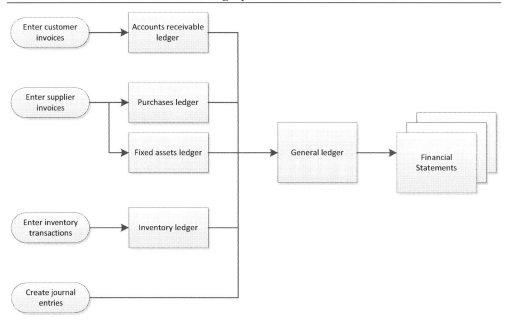

Posting to the General Ledger

Posting refers to the aggregation of financial transactions from where they are stored in subsidiary ledgers, and transferring this information into the general ledger. Information in one of the subsidiary ledgers is aggregated at regular intervals, at which point a summary-level entry is made and posted in the general ledger. In a manual accounting environment, the aggregation may occur at fixed intervals, such as once a day or once a month.

In a computerized bookkeeping environment, posting to the general ledger may be unnoticeable. The software simply does so at regular intervals, or asks if you want to post, and then handles the underlying general ledger posting automatically. It is possible that no posting transaction even appears in the reports generated by the system.

Posting to the general ledger does not occur for lower-volume transactions, which are already recorded in the general ledger. For example, fixed asset purchases may be so infrequent that there is no need for a subsidiary ledger to house these transactions, so they are instead recorded directly in the general ledger.

General Ledger Overview

A general ledger is the master set of accounts in which is summarized all transactions occurring within a business during a specific period of time. The general ledger contains all of the accounts currently being used in a chart of accounts, and is sorted by account number. Either individual transactions or summary-level postings from subsidiary ledgers are listed within each account number, and are sorted by transaction date. Each entry in the general ledger includes a reference number that states the source of the information. The source may be a subsidiary ledger, a journal entry, or a transaction entered directly into the general ledger.

The format of the general ledger varies somewhat, depending on the accounting software being used, but the basic set of information presented for an account within the general ledger is:

- *Transaction number.* The software assigns a unique number to each transaction, so that it can be more easily located in the accounting database if you know the transaction number.
- *Transaction date.* This is the date on which the transaction was entered into the accounting database.
- *Description.* This is a brief description that summarizes the reason for the entry.
- *Source.* Information may be forwarded to the general ledger from a variety of sources, so the report should state the source, in case there is a need to go back to the source to research the reason for the entry.
- *Debit and credit.* States the amount debited or credited to the account for a specific transaction.

The following sample of a general ledger report shows a possible format that could be used to present information for several transactions that are aggregated under a specific account number.

Sample General Ledger Presentation

Trans. No.	Trans. Date	Description	Source	Debit	Credit
Acct. 10400		**Acct: Accounts Receivable**	**Beginning balance**		**$127,500.00**
10473	3/22/xx	Customer invoice	ARL	93.99	
10474	3/23/xx	Customer invoice	ARL	47.80	
10475	3/24/xx	Credit memo	ARL		43.17
10476	3/25/xx	Customer invoice	ARL	65.25	
18903	3/26/xx	Cash receipt	CRJ		1,105.20
			Ending balance		**$126,558.67**

It is extremely easy to locate information pertinent to an accounting inquiry in the general ledger, which makes it the primary source of accounting information. For example:

- A manager reviews the balance sheet and notices that the amount of debt appears too high. The accountant looks up the debt account in the general ledger and sees that a loan was added at the end of the month.
- A manager reviews the income statement and sees that the bad debt expense is very high. The accountant looks up the expense in the general ledger, drills down to the source journal entry, and sees that a new bad debt projection was the cause of the increase in bad debt expense.

As the examples show, the source of an inquiry is frequently the financial statements; when conducting an investigation, the accountant begins with the general ledger, and may drill down to source documents from there to ascertain the reason(s) for an issue.

The Accruals Concept

An accrual is a journal entry that is used to recognize revenues and expenses that have been earned or consumed, respectively, and for which the related source documents have not yet been received or generated. Accruals are needed to ensure that all revenue and expense elements are recognized within the correct reporting period, irrespective of the timing of related cash flows. Without accruals, the amount of revenue, expense, and profit or loss in a period will not necessarily reflect the actual level of economic activity within a business. Accruals are a key part of the closing process used to create financial statements under the accrual basis of accounting; without accruals, financial statements would be considerably less accurate.

It is most efficient to initially record most accruals as reversing entries. This is a useful feature when a business is expecting to issue an invoice to a buyer or receive an invoice from a supplier in the following period. For example, an accountant may know that a supplier invoice for $20,000 will arrive a few days after the end of a month, but she wants to close the books as soon as possible. Accordingly, she records a $20,000 reversing entry to recognize the expense in the current month. In the next month, the accrual reverses, creating a negative $20,000 expense that is offset by the arrival and recordation of the supplier invoice.

Examples of accruals that a business might record are:

- *Expense accrual for interest.* A local lender issues a loan to a business, and sends the borrower an invoice each month, detailing the amount of interest owed. The borrower can record the interest expense in advance of invoice receipt by recording accrued interest.
- *Expense accrual for wages.* An employer pays its employees once a month for the hours they have worked through the 26th day of the month. The employer can accrue all additional wages earned from the 27th through the last day of the month, to ensure that the full amount of the wage expense is recognized.
- *Sales accrual.* A builder has a number of employees working on a major project for the federal government, which it will bill when the project has been completed. In the meantime, the company can accrue revenue for the amount of work completed to date, even though the work has not yet been billed.

If a business records its transactions under the cash basis of accounting, it does not use accruals. Instead, the organization records transactions only when it either pays out or receives cash. See the later Cash Basis of Accounting section for an explanation of this concept.

The Realization Concept

The realization principle is the concept that revenue can only be recognized once the underlying activities associated with the revenue have been delivered or rendered. Thus, revenue can only be recognized after it has been earned. The best way to understand the realization concept is through the following examples:

- *Advance payment for property.* A customer pays $1,000 as a down payment on a parcel of land, but the sale contract has not yet been completed. Since there is not yet a property transfer, the $1,000 is initially recorded as a liability, which is then shifted to revenue only after the sale is complete.
- *Advance payment for services.* A customer pays $6,000 in advance for a full year of property maintenance. The provider does not realize the $6,000 of revenue until it has performed maintenance activities. This can be defined as the passage of time, so the provider could initially record the entire $6,000 as a liability and then shift $500 of it per month to revenue.
- *Delayed payments.* A seller ships goods to a customer on credit, and bills the customer $2,000 for the goods. The seller has realized the entire $2,000 as soon as the shipment has been completed, since there are no additional earning activities to complete. The delayed payment is a financing issue that is unrelated to the realization of revenues.

The realization concept is most often violated when a company wants to accelerate the recognition of revenue, and so books revenues in advance of all related earning activities being completed.

Accrual Basis of Accounting

The accrual basis of accounting is the concept of recording revenues when earned and expenses as incurred. This concept differs from the cash basis of accounting, under which revenues are recorded when cash is received, and expenses are recorded when cash is paid. For example, a company operating under the accrual basis of accounting will record a sale as soon as it issues an invoice to a customer, while a cash basis company would instead wait to be paid before it records the sale. Similarly, an accrual basis company will record an expense as incurred, while a cash basis company would instead wait to pay its supplier before recording the expense.

The accrual basis of accounting is advocated under both the GAAP and IFRS accounting frameworks. Both of these frameworks provide guidance regarding how to account for revenue and expense transactions in the absence of the cash receipts or payments that would trigger the recordation of a transaction under the cash basis of accounting.

The accrual basis tends to provide more even recognition of revenues and expenses over time than the cash basis, and so is considered by investors to be the most valid accounting system for ascertaining the results of operations, financial position, and cash flows of a business. In particular, it supports the matching principle, under which revenues and all related expenses are to be recorded within the same reporting period; by doing so, it should be possible to see the full extent of the profits and losses associated with specific business transactions within a single reporting period.

The accrual basis requires the use of estimated reserves in certain areas. For example, a company should recognize an expense for estimated bad debts that have not yet been incurred. By doing so, all expenses related to a revenue transaction are recorded at the same time as the revenue, which results in an income statement that fully reflects the results of operations. This estimate may not be entirely accurate, and so can lead to materially inaccurate financial statements. Consequently, great care must be used when estimating reserves.

A small business may elect to avoid using the accrual basis of accounting, since it requires a certain amount of accounting expertise. Also, a small business owner may choose to manipulate the timing of cash inflows and outflows to create a smaller amount of taxable income under the cash basis of accounting, which can result in the deferral of income tax payments.

A significant failing of the accrual basis is that it can indicate the presence of profits, even though the associated cash inflows have not yet occurred. The result can be a supposedly profitable entity that is starved for cash, and which may therefore go bankrupt despite its reported level of profitability.

Cash Basis of Accounting

The cash basis of accounting is the practice of only recording revenue when cash is received from a customer, and recording expenses only when cash has been paid out. The cash basis is commonly used by individuals and small businesses. A start-up company will frequently begin keeping its books under the cash basis, and then switch to the accrual basis of accounting (see the preceding section) when it has grown to a sufficient size. The cash basis of accounting has the following advantages:

- *Taxation*. The method is commonly used to record financial results for tax purposes, since a business can accelerate some payments in order to reduce its taxable profits, thereby deferring its tax liability.
- *Ease of use*. A person requires a reduced knowledge of accounting to keep records under the cash basis.

However, the cash basis of accounting also suffers from the following problems:

- *Accuracy*. The cash basis yields less accurate results than the accrual basis of accounting, since the timing of cash flows does not necessarily reflect the proper timing of changes in the financial condition of a business. For example, if a contract with a customer does not allow a business to issue an invoice until the end of a project, the company will be unable to report any revenue until the invoice has been issued and cash received.
- *Manipulation*. A business can alter its reported results by not cashing received checks or altering the payment timing for its liabilities.
- *Lending*. Lenders do not feel that the cash basis generates overly accurate financial statements, and so may refuse to lend money to a business reporting under the cash basis.
- *Audited financial statements*. Auditors will not approve financial statements that were compiled under the cash basis, so a company will need to convert to the accrual basis if it wants to have audited financial statements.
- *Management reporting*. Since the results of cash basis financial statements can be inaccurate, management reports should not be issued that are based upon it.

In short, the numerous problems with the cash basis of accounting usually cause businesses to abandon it after they move beyond their initial startup phases.

EXAMPLE

Masterson Realty owns a warehouse that has a single tenant. The tenant routinely pays the $25,000 monthly rent in a timely manner. In December, the tenant asks if it can pay the next three rent payments in advance, through March of the following year. Masterson accepts this generous offer. Since it uses the cash basis of accounting, Masterson records an additional $75,000 of revenue in the current year.

Consider an alternative scenario, where the tenant complains of having a bad year, and asks if it can defer its final three rent payments until the following year. In this case, Masterson records $75,000 *less* rent in the current year.

Real Estate Financial Statements

Financial statements are a collection of summary-level reports about an organization's financial results, financial position, and cash flows. They are useful for the following reasons:

- To determine the ability of a business to generate cash, and the sources and uses of that cash.
- To determine whether a business has the capability to pay back its debts.
- To track financial results on a trend line to spot any looming profitability issues.
- To derive financial ratios from the statements that can indicate the condition of the business.
- To investigate the details of certain business transactions, as outlined in the disclosures that accompany the statements.

The standard contents of a set of financial statements are:

- *Balance sheet*. Shows the entity's assets, liabilities, and stockholders' equity as of the report date. It does not show information that covers a span of time.
- *Income statement*. Shows the results of the entity's operations and financial activities for the reporting period. It includes revenues, expenses, gains, and losses.
- *Statement of cash flows*. Shows changes in the entity's cash flows during the reporting period.

The line items used in financial statements can vary significantly by industry. That being the case, we have included sample financial statements for a real estate business in the following exhibits.

Sample Income Statement

	20X1
Rental Revenue:	$2,800,000
Expenses:	
Advertising	10,000
Amortization	25,000
Cleaning	110,000
Depreciation	390,000
Elevator	2,000
Equipment rental	3,000
Ground rent	50,000
Insurance	20,000
Interest – mortgage	1,000,000
Legal and professional	25,000
Management fees	80,000
Office expense	15,000
Real estate taxes	420,000
Repairs and maintenance	250,000
Utilities	590,000
Total Expenses	2,990,000
Excess of Expenses over Revenues	-190,000
Capital Contribution	240,000
Ending Members' Equity	$5,720,000

Sample Balance Sheet

	20X1
Rental Property:	
Land	$4,000,000
Building and improvements	19,000,000
Equipment	100,000
Total	23,100,000
Less: Accumulated depreciation	1,500,000
	21,600,000
Other Assets:	
Cash	90,000
Rents receivable	40,000
Prepaid expenses	50,000
Escrow	260,000
Intangible assets, net of accumulated amortization	300,000
Total other assets	740,000
Total Assets	**$22,340,000**
Liabilities:	
Mortgage payable	$16,000,000
Accounts payable and accrued expenses	540,000
Tenant security deposits	80,000
Total Liabilities	16,620,000
Members' Equity	5,720,000
Total Liabilities and Members' Equity	**$22,340,000**

Sample Statement of Cash Flows

	20X1
Cash Flows from Operating Activities:	
Excess of expenses over revenues	-$190,000
Depreciation	390,000
Amortization	25,000
Net change in operating assets and liabilities	
Rents receivable	-20,000
Escrow	-200,000
Accounts payable	80,000
Net cash provided by operating activities	85,000
Cash Flows from Investing Activities:	
Purchase of building improvements	-280,000
Payment of leasing commissions	-10,000
Net cash used by investing activities	-290,000
Cash Flows from Financing Activities:	
Proceeds from mortgage	135,000
Financing costs	-190,000
Capital contributions	240,000
Net cash provided by financing activities	185,000
Net Decrease in Cash	-20,000
Cash – Beginning	110,000
Cash – Ending	$90,000

Real Estate Entities

There are a number of possible legal entities that can be used to own real estate. Each one imposes different risks and protections on its owners, while also offering different types of tax benefits and obligations. Also, the type of entity chosen can impact the level of control that investors have over the operations of the entity. Consequently, one should have a firm concept of the advantages and disadvantages of each type of legal entity, which we address in the following sub-sections.

Sole Proprietorship

A sole proprietorship is a business that is directly owned by a single individual. It is not incorporated, so that the sole owner is entitled to the entire net worth of the business, and is personally liable for its debts. The individual and the business are considered to be the same entity for tax purposes. The advantages of a sole proprietorship are:

- *Simple to organize.* The initial organization of the business is quite simple. At most, the owner might reserve a business name with the secretary of state. It is also quite easy to upgrade to other forms of organization.
- *Simple tax filings.* The owner does not have to file a separate income tax return for the business. Instead, the results of the business are listed on a separate schedule of the individual income tax return (Form 1040).
- *No double taxation.* There is no double taxation, as can be the case in a corporation, where earnings are taxed at the corporate level and then distributed to owners via dividends, where they are taxed again. Instead, earnings flow straight to the owner.
- *Complete control.* There is only one owner, who has absolute control over the direction of the business and how its resources are allocated.

The disadvantages of a sole proprietorship are as follows:

- *Unlimited liability.* The chief disadvantage is that the owner is entirely liable for any losses incurred by the business, with no limitation. For example, the owner may invest $1,000 in a real estate venture, which then incurs net obligations of $100,000. The owner is personally liable for the entire $100,000. An adequate amount of liability insurance and risk management practices can mitigate this concern.
- *Self-employment taxes.* The owner is liable for a 15.3% self-employment tax (social security and Medicare) on all earnings generated by the business that are not exempt from these taxes. There is a cap on the social security portion of this tax ($118,500 in 2015). There is no cap on the Medicare rate – instead, the rate *increases* by 0.9% at certain threshold levels.
- *No outside equity.* The only provider of equity to the business is the sole owner. Funding usually comes from personal savings and debt for which the owner is liable. For a large increase in capital, the owner would likely need to use a different organizational structure that would admit multiple owners.

This form of business is commonly used for individual and small multi-family residential properties. The unlimited liability aspect of the sole proprietorship limits its use to smaller investments.

Partnership

A partnership is a form of business organization in which owners have unlimited personal liability for the actions of the business, though this problem can be mitigated through the use of a limited liability partnership. The owners of a partnership have invested their own funds and time in the business, and share proportionally in any profits earned by it. There may also be limited partners in the business, who contribute funds but do not take part in day-to-day operations. A limited partner is only liable for the amount of funds he or she invested in the business; once those funds are paid out, the limited partner has no additional liability in relation to the activities of the partnership. If there are limited partners, there must also be a designated general partner that is an active manager of the business; this individual has essentially the same liabilities as a sole proprietor.

A partnership agreement is a written or oral agreement that governs decision making within a partnership, as well as how key decisions are handled. A partnership agreement should include information or provide instructions about the following topics:

- The names of the partners
- The amounts contributed by each partner
- The rights and responsibilities of each partner
- Whether partners are designated as general partners or limited partners
- The proportions of partnership gains and losses to be apportioned to each partner
- Procedures related to the withdrawal of funds from the partnership, as well as any limitations on these withdrawals
- How key decisions are to be resolved
- Provisions regarding how to add partners and terminate partners
- What happens to partnership interests if a partner dies
- What steps to follow to dissolve the partnership

If a partnership agreement does not include the preceding topics, then there is a risk of acrimony among the partners when a decision must be made, and there is no formal guidance regarding how to proceed.

A partnership does not pay income taxes. Instead, the various partners report their share of the partnership's profit on their personal income tax returns.

The primary tax form filed by a partnership is the Form 1065. This form notes the amount of taxable income generated by the partnership, and the amount of this income attributable to each of the partners. In addition, the partnership issues a Schedule K-1 to each of the partners, on which is stated the amount of partnership income attributed to them, and which they should include on their own personal income tax returns.

Because partners must pay income taxes on their shares of partnership income, they typically require some distribution of cash from the partnership in order to pay their taxes. If a partner elects to instead leave some portion of his or her share of a distribution in the partnership, this is considered an incremental increase in the capital contribution of that person to the business.

In those instances where a partnership recognizes a loss during its fiscal year, the share of the loss recognized by each partner in his or her personal tax return is limited to the amount of the loss that offsets each partner's basis in the partnership. If the amount of the loss is greater than this basis, the excess amount must be carried forward into a future period, where it can hopefully be offset against the future profits of the partnership. In essence, tax law does not allow a partner to recognize more on his or her tax return than the amount contributed into a partnership.

The key advantages of a partnership are as follows:

- *Source of capital*. With many partners, a business has a much richer source of capital than would be the case for a sole proprietorship.
- *Specialization*. If there is more than one general partner, it is possible for multiple people with diverse skill sets to run a business, which can enhance its overall performance.
- *Minimal tax filings*. The Form 1065 that a partnership must file is not a complicated tax filing.
- *No double taxation*. There is no double taxation, as can be the case in a corporation. Instead, earnings flow straight to the owners.

The disadvantages of a partnership are as follows:

- *Unlimited liability*. The general partners have unlimited personal liability for the obligations of the partnership, as was the case with a sole proprietorship. This is a joint and several liability, which means that creditors can pursue a single general partner for the obligations of the entire business.
- *Self-employment taxes*. A partner's share of the ordinary income reported on a Schedule K-1 is subject to the self-employment tax noted earlier for a sole proprietorship.

Corporation

A corporation is a legal entity, organized under state laws, whose investors purchase shares of stock as evidence of their ownership in it. A corporation can potentially exist indefinitely. It also acts as a legal shield for its owners, so that they are generally not liable for the corporation's actions. A corporation pays all types of taxes, including income taxes, payroll taxes, sales and use taxes, and property taxes.

A private company has a small group of investors who are unable to sell their shares to the general public. A public company has registered its shares for sale with the Securities and Exchange Commission (SEC), and may also have listed its shares on an exchange, where they can be traded by the general public. The requirements of the SEC and the stock exchanges are rigorous, so comparatively few corporations are publicly-held.

The advantages of the corporation are as follows:

- *Limited liability*. The shareholders of a corporation are only liable up to the amount of their investments. The corporate entity shields them from any further liability.
- *Source of capital*. A publicly-held corporation in particular can raise substantial amounts by selling shares or issuing bonds.

- *Ownership transfers.* It is not especially difficult for a shareholder to sell shares in a corporation, though this is more difficult when the entity is privately-held.

The disadvantages of a corporation are as follows:

- *Double taxation.* Depending on the type of corporation, it may pay taxes on its income, after which shareholders pay taxes on any dividends received, so income can be taxed twice.
- *Excessive tax filings.* Depending on the type of corporation, the various types of income and other taxes that must be paid can add up to a substantial amount of paperwork.

There are two main types of corporation, which are the C corporation and S corporation.

C Corporation

The default form of corporation is the C corporation. It is taxed as a separate entity, for which the tax filing can be voluminous. Distributions to shareholders are made at the discretion of the board of directors of the company, in the form of dividends. A dividend is considered taxable income to the recipient (though it is not subject to self-employment taxes). This means that there *is* double taxation, where the corporation pays an income tax on its earnings, and shareholders also pay a tax on dividends received. Despite the double taxation disadvantage, the C corporation structure is heavily used, because it can be owned by an unlimited number of shareholders. This gives it an unrivaled ability to attract capital from investors.

EXAMPLE

Whitestone Realty sells a property for a gain of $1,000,000. Whitestone will pay income tax on the taxable gain. In addition, it distributes a $1,000,000 dividend to its shareholders, who will pay personal income tax on it. Whitestone's tax rate is 21% and its shareholders are subject to the maximum income tax rate of 37%, so the aggregate tax percentage applicable to the $1,000,000 gain is 58%.

S Corporation

A variation on the standard corporation model is the S corporation. An S corporation passes its income through to its owners, so that the entity itself does not pay income taxes. The owners report the income on their tax returns, thereby avoiding the double taxation that arises in a regular C corporation. Some additional points regarding the S corporation are:

- There can be no more than 100 shareholders, so this approach is most suitable for smaller entities.

- All of the shareholders must agree to adopt the S corporation structure.
- Every shareholder must be a United States resident or citizen.
- A C corporation or a partnership cannot be a shareholder, though estates and certain trusts and charities can be investors.
- There can only be a single class of stock, which prevents preferential payments and voting privileges.

An S corporation may still have to pay taxes under a few circumstances, which include:

- It has accumulated earnings from an earlier time period as a C corporation, and at least 25% of its gross receipts are from passive income
- It has certain types of capital gains
- It has recaptured an investment tax credit

If the owners or management of an S corporation want to switch to a different organizational structure, more than 50% of the shareholders must agree to this in writing. There must also be a statement by the entity, pointing out the same intent.

Limited Liability Company

A limited liability company (LLC) combines the features of corporations and partnerships, which makes them an ideal entity for many businesses. Their advantages are:

- *Limited liability*. The liability of investors is limited to the amount of their investments in the LLC. They are also shielded from the actions of the LLC.
- *Income flow through*. An LLC can be structured so that the income earned by the business flows directly through to investors. This means that the investors pay income taxes, rather than the LLC. When there are multiple investors, each will receive a Schedule K-1 for reporting their pro rata share of the LLC's profit or loss on their individual tax returns.
- *Management*. An LLC can be run by professional managers, rather than a general partner.
- *Paperwork*. The level of recordkeeping is less than for a corporation.
- *Number of investors*. There is no limitation on the number of investors in an LLC, as opposed to the maximum cap on an S corporation.
- *Multiple classes of stock*. An LLC can issue multiple classes of stock, which can be useful when providing special privileges to certain investors.

The disadvantages of an LLC include:

- *Differing structures*. Each state has implemented different rules regarding how an LLC is structured and operated. This can cause confusion regarding the risks to which investors are subjected, how the entity can be managed, and its tax effects.

- *Filing fees.* There will be annual government fees charged to maintain an LLC entity, though the amount may not be excessive (depending on the state).
- *Fund raising.* It can be difficult for an LLC to obtain funding, since investors may be put off by this somewhat obscure entity type.

Real Estate Investment Trust

A real estate investment trust (REIT) is a real estate company that sells its common stock to the public; its shares trade on a stock exchange. An REIT manages a number of income-producing properties, such as shopping malls, industrial properties, and hotels. It is required to distribute most of its profits in the form of dividends to shareholders. The operating requirements for an REIT are:

- A minimum of 75% of its gross income must come in some way from income related to real estate.
- Five or fewer persons cannot own a majority of the REIT stock value.
- It is not allowed to reinvest its earnings.
- It must distribute at least 90% of its capital gains from the sale of property.
- It must distribute at least 90% of its ordinary income to shareholders as a dividend.
- It must have a minimum of 100 shareholders.
- It must use independent contractors to manage the properties it owns.

Tiered Partnerships

A key consideration for the real estate investor is to protect each property from claims against other properties. For example, if one property has substantial claims against it, all other assets held within the same entity will also be subject to the claims of those creditors. This can be avoided with a tiered partnership structure, where all funds are invested in a holding company; this company then creates a separate LLC for each property owned, and invests enough money into each LLC to fund the required asset purchases. Each LLC then makes cash distributions back to the holding company, which in turn issues dividends to investors.

EXAMPLE

Investors put $55 million into Great Lakes Holding Company, which invests $10 million of this amount into a parking garage, $30 million into an office building, and the remaining $15 million into an apartment complex. Each investment is made through a separate LLC. After a year, it is apparent that major layoffs at a nearby employer are causing the tenancy rate at the apartment complex to decline sharply, making it difficult to pay creditor invoices. These creditor claims cannot be extended to the parking garage or the office building, since those properties are owned by separate LLC entities.

The Following Chapters

The following chapters delve into considerable detail regarding specific accounting transactions as they relate to real estate events. These chapters are based upon the Generally Accepted Accounting Principles framework. The general flow of these chapters is to begin with the costs incurred as part of a real estate development project or the purchase of an income-producing property, followed by its sale to a third party. There are several variations on the concept of a sale, including the sale of real estate, retail land sales, and nonmonetary exchanges of property. Beyond these basic activities, we use several additional chapters to cover more specific activities and entities related to real estate, including:

- Time-sharing intervals
- Rent topics
- Asset retirement and environmental obligations
- Real estate ventures
- Housing associations

Summary

This chapter primarily focused on how business transactions are recorded in the accounting database. The level of detail given was intended to provide the reader with a basic understanding of the process. This will be of use in the following chapters, as we delve into the specific details of real estate accounting. For more information about accounting in general, see the author's *Bookkeeping Guidebook*, *Accountants' Guidebook*, and *Closing the Books*.

Chapter 2
Initial Real Estate Costs

Introduction

The accounting for real estate begins with the initial investment in a property. This could be a simple purchase of an existing property, or could involve something more complex – a developer might create entire structures on undeveloped land. In the latter case, many types of costs may be involved, including permitting, interest costs, and architectural design fees. In addition, these costs may be incurred before a project has even been finalized, and so are at risk of never contributing to the completion of a finished project.

Given the potential complexity of these initial real estate costs, the accountant is faced with many decisions regarding whether to charge them to expense immediately, or to capitalize them into the cost of a real estate project. In this chapter, we explore how each cost should be treated. Accounting for the purchase of an existing income-producing property is addressed in the next chapter.

Relevant Accounting Sources

The information stated in this chapter is derived from the following topics in the Accounting Standards Codification (which is a summary of Generally Accepted Accounting Principles):

- Topic 340, *Other Assets and Deferred Costs*
- Topic 835, *Interest*
- Topic 970, *Real Estate – General*

Capitalization

We have noted that the accountant must decide whether to charge an initial real estate cost to expense as soon as it is incurred, or to capitalize it. What is capitalization? It is the recognition of a cost as an asset. In relation to real estate, this means that capitalized costs are associated with a specific project, such that an asset exists in the developer's balance sheet for that project. These costs are accumulated until a project is complete, at which point there are two possible alternatives for how to treat the asset:

- The completed project is sold, in which case the capitalized cost is charged to the cost of goods sold in the same period in which revenue is recognized, resulting in the developer recognizing either a profit or loss on the sale; or
- The developer retains and uses the completed property, in which case the real estate is classified as a fixed asset and is depreciated over its useful life.

Real Estate Preacquisition Costs

An investor may make expenditures related to a specific property, but before actually acquiring it. These costs are known as preacquisition costs. Examples of these costs are noted in the following table.

Examples of Preacquisition Costs

Appraisal fees	Legal fees
Architectural design fees	Purchase option cost
Engineering fees	Surveying fees
Environmental study fees	Title searches
Feasibility study fees	Traffic study fees

Treatment of Preacquisition Costs

The essential rules for when to capitalize preacquisition costs are as follows:

- *Purchase option cost.* An investor may purchase an option to acquire real property. If so, the cost of the option should be capitalized at once.
- *Other costs that can be capitalized.* Other preacquisition costs can be capitalized if they meet the following conditions:
  - The costs are directly associated with a specific property.
  - It is probable that the investor will acquire either the property or an option to acquire it. A transaction is only considered to be probable if the following conditions are present:
    - The investor is actively working to acquire the property;
    - The investor can obtain financing for the acquisition; and
    - The property is available for sale.

If a pre-acquisition cost does not meet the preceding conditions, it should instead be charged to expense as incurred.

A number of preacquisition costs are never capitalized. Instead, they are considered to be the ongoing cost of the operations of the real estate developer, and so should be charged to expense as incurred. Examples of these costs are:

- Costs incurred to identify commercial properties
- Costs to negotiate for and acquire commercial properties

EXAMPLE

Dude Sports develops and operates sporting goods stores. Its property development group is searching for its next store location, and has paid for traffic studies in five areas to determine which one will generate the most foot traffic. The cost of these studies is $50,000.

Dude cannot capitalize the cost of these studies, since it is not yet probable that a property will be acquired. Instead, the costs must be charged to expense as incurred.

As just noted in the requirements for capitalization, it must be probable that the investor will acquire a property. This does not mean that the property *will* be acquired with absolute certainty. If circumstances later result in the investor *not* acquiring the property, then all of the previously-capitalized costs associated with that property should be charged to expense at once.

Conversely, if the investor *does* acquire the property, then the previously-capitalized costs should be rolled into the project costs for the property.

Operating and Non-Operating Classifications

A property is considered to be operating when there is no further major construction activity, and it is either producing income already, or is available for occupancy as soon as tenant improvements have been made by the acquirer.

If preacquisition costs have been capitalized and the developer subsequently determines that the property should be classified as operating as of the acquisition date, these costs should be charged to expense at once. Also, any additional acquisition costs should be charged to expense as incurred.

Conversely, if preacquisition costs have already been charged to expense and the developer subsequently determines that the property should be classified as non-operating, it is not allowable to capitalize these costs after the fact. Instead, they must remain expensed.

Internally-Generated Preacquisition Costs

A real estate developer may have an acquisitions and development group that routinely locates and develops new properties. The costs incurred by this group are normally classified as routine operating costs, which are charged to expense as incurred.

Internally-generated preacquisition costs can be capitalized, but only if they relate to a specific property, and that property will not be operational at the time of the acquisition. Conversely, all preacquisition costs incurred in association with a property acquisition should be charged to expense as incurred if the property will be operating as of the acquisition date.

Real Estate Project Costs

Once a property has been acquired, the accountant's next concern is to determine the proper treatment of expenditures related to the associated project. A real estate project is activities related to the conversion of real estate into the final income-producing form envisioned by the developer. Project costs are those costs directly related to the acquisition and construction of a real estate project. For example, costs may be incurred to drain swamp land, install a parking lot and develop trails in order to create a botanical center.

In general, project costs are to be capitalized if they are clearly associated with the acquisition, development, or construction of a real estate project. Examples of these costs are noted in the following table, with direct and indirect project costs noted in separate columns.

Sample Project Costs

Direct Project Costs	Indirect Project Costs
Commissions	Construction administration costs
Construction costs	Construction crew compensation
Demolition costs	Construction equipment depreciation costs
Engineering fees	Planning staff costs
Environmental remediation costs	Project cost accounting
Insurance billings incurred during construction	
Permitting fees	
Property purchase price	
Property recordation fees	
Property taxes incurred during construction	
Title search fees	

Direct project costs are those costs that are directly related to the acquisition, development, and/or construction of a specific property, while indirect costs clearly relate to multiple projects currently under development. General and administrative expenses that relate to no projects at all are to be charged to expense as incurred. Examples of general and administrative expenses are noted in the following table.

Sample General and Administrative Expenses

Administrative staff compensation	Human resources
Audit fees	Legal fees
Building rent	Non-project accounting
Consulting fees	Non-project insurance
Corporate management compensation	Office equipment depreciation
Corporate marketing	Office supplies
Facility depreciation	Subscriptions
Facility utilities	Utilities

Real Estate Taxes and Property Insurance

During the period when a property is being prepared for its intended use, it is acceptable to capitalize real estate taxes and property insurance. After the property is ready for its intended use, all subsequent real estate taxes and property insurance are charged to expense as incurred.

There may be cases in which only a portion of a property is being actively developed. If so, only capitalize these costs for that portion of the property that is under development. All real estate taxes and property insurance related to the remainder of the property should be charged to expense as incurred.

EXAMPLE

Historical Battle Enterprises buys 50,000 acres of real estate in Narcoossee, located just south of Orlando, Florida. The company hopes to expand on the town's existing annual re-enactment of the Battle at Narcoossee Mill by creating a variety of historical battles that adults can either view or participate in – for a fee. The company is currently converting 5,000 acres of swampland on its new property into a lake battle re-enactment of the Battle of Salamis, between the Greeks and Persians.

The company receives annual billings totaling $1,000,000 for real estate taxes. It is reasonable to capitalize 10% of this amount, which corresponds to that portion of the property actively under development (as a proportion of total acreage). The remainder is charged to expense.

Real Estate Interest Costs

A larger real estate development project can require substantial debt funding, for which the associated interest cost can be significant. It is allowable to capitalize the cost of the interest incurred during the property development period. This section describes the assets for which interest capitalization is allowable (or not), how to determine the capitalization period and the capitalization rate, and how to calculate the amount of interest cost to be capitalized.

Interest is a cost of doing business, and if a developer incurs an interest cost that is directly related to a project, it is reasonable to capitalize this cost, since it provides a truer picture of the total investment in the project. Since the developer would not otherwise have incurred the interest if it had not acquired the property, the interest is essentially a direct cost of owning the real estate.

Conversely, if a developer were not to capitalize the cost of interest and instead charged it to expense, this would unreasonably reduce the amount of reported earnings during the period when the developer incurred the expense, and increase earnings during later periods, when it would otherwise have been charging the capitalized interest to expense through depreciation.

The value of the information provided by capitalizing interest may not be worth the effort of the incremental accounting cost associated with it. Here are some issues to consider when deciding whether to capitalize interest:

- How many projects would be subject to interest capitalization?
- How easy is it to separately identify those projects that would be subject to interest capitalization?
- How significant would be the effect of interest capitalization on the developer's reported resources and earnings?

Thus, only capitalize interest when the informational benefit derived from doing so exceeds the cost of accounting for it. The positive impact of doing so is greatest for construction projects, where:

- Costs are separately compiled
- Construction covers a long period of time
- Expenditures are large
- Interest costs are considerable

Assets for Which Interest Must be Capitalized

Capitalize interest that is related to the following types of property:

- Assets that are constructed for the company's own use. This includes assets built for the company by suppliers, where the company makes progress payments or deposits.
- Assets that are constructed for sale or lease, and which are constructed as discrete projects.

EXAMPLE

Milford Sound builds a new corporate headquarters. The company hires a contractor to perform the work, and makes regular progress payments to the contractor. Milford should capitalize the interest expense related to this project.

Milford Sound creates a subsidiary, Milford Public Sound, which builds custom-designed outdoor sound staging for concerts and theatre activities. These projects require many months to complete, and are accounted for as discrete projects. Milford should capitalize the interest cost related to each of these projects.

If a developer is undertaking activities to develop land for a specific use, capitalize interest related to the associated expenditures for as long as the development activities are in progress.

Assets for Which Interest is not Capitalized

Do not capitalize interest that is related to the following types of fixed assets:

- Properties that are already in use or ready for their intended use
- Properties not being used, and which are not being prepared for use
- Properties not included in the developer's balance sheet

The Interest Capitalization Period

Capitalize interest over the period when there are ongoing activities to prepare a project for its intended use, but only if expenditures are actually being made during that time, and interest costs are being incurred.

EXAMPLE

Milford Public Sound is constructing an in-house sound stage in which to test its products. It spent the first two months designing the stage, and then paid a contractor $30,000 per month for the next four months to build the stage. Milford incurred interest costs during the entire time period.

Since Milford was not making any expenditures related to the stage during the first two months, it cannot capitalize any interest cost for those two months. However, since it was making expenditures during the next four months, it can capitalize interest cost for those months.

If essentially all construction on a project is halted, stop capitalizing interest during that period. However, continue to capitalize interest under any of the following circumstances:

- Brief construction interruptions
- Interruptions imposed by an outside entity
- Delays that are an inherent part of the asset acquisition process

---

EXAMPLE

Milford Public Sound is constructing a concert arena that it plans to lease to a local municipality upon completion. Midway through the project, the municipality orders a halt to all construction, when construction reveals that the arena is being built on an Indian burial ground. Two months later, after the burial site has been relocated, the municipality allows construction to begin again.

Since this interruption was imposed by an outside entity, Milford can capitalize interest during the two-month stoppage period.

Terminate interest capitalization as soon as an asset is substantially complete and ready for its intended use. Here are several scenarios showing when to terminate interest capitalization:

- *Unit-level completion*. Parts of a project may be completed and usable before the entire project is complete. Stop capitalizing interest on each of these parts as soon as they are substantially complete and ready for use.
- *Entire-unit completion*. All aspects of a project may need to be completed before any part of it can be used. Continue capitalizing interest on such assets until the entire project is substantially complete and ready for use.
- *Dependent completion*. An asset may not be usable until a separate project has also been completed. Continue capitalizing interest on such assets until not only the specific asset, but also the separate project is substantially complete and ready for use.

EXAMPLE

Milford Public Sound is building three arenas, all under different circumstances. They are:

1. *Arena A*. This is an entertainment complex, including a stage area, movie theatre, and restaurants. Milford should stop capitalizing interest on each component of the project as soon as it is substantially complete and ready for use, since each part of the complex can operate without the other parts being complete.
2. *Arena B*. This is a single outdoor stage with integrated multi-level parking garage. Even though the garage is completed first, Milford should continue to capitalize interest for it, since the garage is only intended to service patrons of the arena, and so will not be operational until the arena is complete.
3. *Arena C*. This an entertainment complex for which Milford is also constructing a highway off-ramp and road that leads to the complex. Since the complex is unusable until patrons can reach the complex, Milford should continue to capitalize interest expenses until the off-ramp and road are complete.

Do not continue to capitalize interest when completion is being deliberately delayed, since the cost of interest then changes from an asset acquisition cost to an asset holding cost.

EXAMPLE

The CEO of Milford Sound wants to report increased net income for the upcoming quarter, so he orders the delay of construction on an arena facility that would otherwise have been completed, so that the interest cost related to the project will be capitalized. He is in error, since this is now treated as a holding cost – the related interest expense should be recognized in the period incurred, rather than capitalized.

The Capitalization Rate

The amount of interest cost to capitalize for a project is that amount of interest that would have been avoided if the developer had not acquired the property. To calculate the amount of interest cost to capitalize, multiply the capitalization rate by the average amount of expenditures that accumulate during the construction period.

The basis for the capitalization rate is the interest rates that are applicable to the developer's borrowings that are outstanding during the construction period. If a specific borrowing is incurred in order to construct a specific asset, use the interest rate on that borrowing as the capitalization rate. If the amount of a specific borrowing that is incurred to construct a specific asset is less than the expenditures made for the asset, use a weighted average of the rates applicable to other developer borrowings for any excess expenditures over the amount of the project-specific borrowing.

EXAMPLE

Milford Public Sound incurs an average expenditure over the construction period of an outdoor arena complex of $15,000,000. It has taken out a short-term loan of $12,000,000 at 9% interest specifically to cover the cost of this project. Milford can capitalize the interest cost of the entire amount of the $12,000,000 loan at 9% interest, but it still has $3,000,000 of average expenditures that exceed the amount of this project-specific loan.

Milford has two bonds outstanding at the time of the project, in the following amounts:

Bond Description	Principal Outstanding	Interest
8% Bond	$18,000,000	$1,440,000
10% Bond	12,000,000	1,200,000
Totals	$30,000,000	$2,640,000

The weighted-average interest rate on these two bond issuances is 8.8% ($2,640,000 interest ÷ $30,000,000 principal), which is the interest rate that Milford should use when capitalizing the remaining $3,000,000 of average expenditures.

These rules regarding the formulation of the capitalization rate are subject to some interpretation. The key guideline is to arrive at a *reasonable* measure of the cost of financing the acquisition of a fixed asset, particularly in regard to the interest cost that could have been avoided if the acquisition had not been made. Thus, one can use a selection of outstanding borrowings as the basis for a weighted average calculation. This may result in the inclusion or exclusion of borrowings at the corporate level, or just at the level of the subsidiary where the asset is located.

EXAMPLE

Milford Public Sound (MPS) has issued several bonds and notes, totaling $50,000,000, that are used to fund both general corporate activities and construction projects. It also has access to a low-cost 4% internal line of credit that is extended to it by its corporate parent, Milford Sound. MPS regularly uses this line of credit for short-term activities, and typically draws the balance down to zero at least once a year. The average amount of this line that is outstanding is approximately $10,000,000 at any given time.

Since the corporate line of credit comprises a significant amount of MPS's ongoing borrowings, and there is no restriction that prevents these funds from being used for construction projects, it would be reasonable to include the interest cost of this line of credit in the calculation of the weighted-average cost of borrowings that is used to derive MPS's capitalization rate.

Calculating Interest Capitalization

Follow these steps to calculate the amount of interest to be capitalized for a specific project:

1. Construct a table itemizing the amounts of expenditures made and the dates on which the expenditures were made.
2. Determine the date on which interest capitalization ends.
3. Calculate the capitalization period for each expenditure, which is the number of days between the specific expenditure and the end of the interest capitalization period.
4. Divide each capitalization period by the total number of days elapsed between the date of the first expenditure and the end of the interest capitalization period to arrive at the capitalization multiplier for each line item.
5. Multiply each expenditure amount by its capitalization multiplier to arrive at the average expenditure for each line item over the capitalization measurement period.
6. Add up the average expenditures at the line item level to arrive at a grand total average expenditure.
7. If there is project-specific debt, multiply the grand total of the average expenditures by the interest rate on that debt to arrive at the capitalized interest related to that debt.
8. If the grand total of the average expenditures exceeds the amount of the project-specific debt, multiply the excess expenditure amount by the weighted average of the company's other outstanding debt to arrive at the remaining amount of interest to be capitalized.
9. Add together both capitalized interest calculations. If the combined total is more than the total interest cost incurred by the company during the calculation period, reduce the amount of interest to be capitalized to the total interest cost incurred by the company during the calculation period.
10. Record the interest capitalization with a debit to the project's asset account and a credit to the interest expense account.

EXAMPLE

Milford Public Sound is building a concert arena. Milford makes payments related to the project of $10,000,000 and $14,000,000 to a contractor on January 1 and July 1, respectively. The arena is completed on December 31.

For the 12-month period of construction, Milford can capitalize all of the interest on the $10,000,000 payment, since it was outstanding during the full period of construction. Milford can capitalize the interest on the $14,000,000 payment for half of the construction period, since it was outstanding during only the second half of the construction period. The average expenditure for which the interest cost can be capitalized is calculated in the following table.

Date of Payment	Expenditure Amount	Capitalization Period*	Capitalization Multiplier	Average Expenditure
January 1	$10,000,000	12 months	12/12 months = 100%	$10,000,000
July 1	14,000,000	6 months	6/12 months = 50%	7,000,000
				$17,000,000

* In the table, the capitalization period is defined as the number of months that elapse between the expenditure payment date and the end of the interest capitalization period.

The only debt that Milford has outstanding during this period is a line of credit, on which the interest rate is 8%. The maximum amount of interest that Milford can capitalize into the cost of this arena project is $1,360,000, which is calculated as:

8% Interest rate × $17,000,000 Average expenditure = $1,360,000

Milford records the following journal entry:

	Debit	Credit
Fixed assets – Arena	1,360,000	
Interest expense		1,360,000

Tip: There may be an inordinate number of expenditures related to a larger project, which could result in a large and unwieldy calculation of average expenditures. To reduce the workload, consider aggregating these expenses by month, and then assume that each expenditure was made in the middle of the month, thereby reducing all of the expenditures for each month to a single line item.

It is not permissible to capitalize more interest cost in an accounting period than the total amount of interest cost incurred by the developer in that period. If there is a corporate parent, this rule means that the amount capitalized cannot exceed the total amount of interest cost incurred by the business on a consolidated basis.

Impact of Financing on Property Purchase Price

A common element of many real estate transactions is that the seller provides financing to the buyer. It is possible that this financing will include an interest rate that does not match the current market rate, or that the stated amount of the note plus any down payment differs from the cash prices being paid for similar properties. In either case, the property purchase price should be recorded by the buyer at an amount that reflects the more determinable of either:

- The fair value of the property; or
- The market value of the note plus any other consideration paid to the seller.

If the buyer is using the latter option and it is not possible to find a market value for the note, instead use an imputed interest rate to calculate the present value of all future payments associated with the note. This imputed rate should be the prevailing rate for similar borrowers with similar credit ratings, which may be further adjusted for the following factors:

- The credit standing of the borrower
- Restrictive covenants on the note
- Collateral on the note
- Tax consequences to the buyer and seller
- The rate at which the borrower can obtain similar financing from other sources

Once the correct interest rate has been selected, use it to amortize the difference between the imputed interest rate and the rate on the note over the life of the note, with the difference being charged to the interest expense account.

Costs Allocated to Real Estate Projects

A developer may purchase a property and then develop it over a long period of time, gradually adding new phases to the project as old phases are completed and sold. If so, it is essential to formally recognize separate phases within the overall project. Otherwise, capitalized costs relating to an early phase might be incorrectly allocated to a part of a project that will not be completed for years; this would result in the reporting of excessive profit levels in the earlier reporting periods of a project.

There are a number of ways to distinguish the phases of a project for cost assignment purposes, including the following:

- Units that have been linked to a real estate owners' association
- Units that the property developer has declared to be for sale
- Units expected to be constructed during a specific period of time

---

EXAMPLE

Princeville Development has purchased a 2,000 acre property on the island of Kauai. The project is expected to encompass several phases that include a cluster of single-family residences, several hundred condominiums, a small retail shopping center, and a hotel. Possible allocation scenarios for Princeville to consider are:

- $1,000,000 for access roads. This expenditure benefits all phases of the project, and so can be allocated across all phases.
- $150,000 for parking lots for the shopping center and hotel. This expenditure should not be allocated to the residences or condominiums, since it only benefits the shopping center and hotel.
- $400,000 for utility lines into the condominium complex. These costs only benefit the condominium units, and so should be allocated only to them.

When the costs of a real estate project have been capitalized, they should then be allocated to individual components of the project. Whenever possible, this allocation is to be based on the specific identification of a cost with a project component, which results in the most accurate cost allocation. Such an allocation is known as the *specific identification method*. If this is not practicable, capitalized costs should be allocated in the following order:

1. The costs of land and all common costs are to be allocated to land parcels based on their relative fair values before construction. This is called the *relative value method*.
2. The costs of construction are to be allocated to individual units in each phase based on their relative sales values. This is a variation on the relative value method.
3. If an allocation based on relative value is impracticable, allocate capitalized costs on an appropriate *area method* or value method. An area method is an allocation based on the square footage of a lot or structure, or the number of units in a project phase.

EXAMPLE

The Apollo Development Group buys a parcel of land, on which it plans to build an air and space museum, hotel, and restaurant. Apollo can allocate the cost of the land based on the estimated relative fair values of the museum, hotel, and restaurant.

Moccasin Partners constructs a parking garage to provide for the parking needs of a condominium complex that it is also constructing. Moccasin can allocate the cost of the garage to the individual condominium units, based on their relative sales values.

Literal Corporation is building a warehouse that will house a large number of small storage facilities. Literal can allocate the cost of partition construction to each storage facility based on their relative square footage.

The assumptions used to make allocations between the various phases of a project should be reviewed at regular intervals, since they may change. For example, the relative sales values of the units in a project may change over time, which will alter the costs allocated to them under the relative value method. This is a normal part of the accounting for longer-term development projects.

Real Estate Donated to the Government

A real estate developer may donate land to a municipality, for example as open space. This type of donation benefits the project, since it protects adjacent land from further development. In such cases, the cost of the donated real estate is considered a common cost of the project, and so is allocated as a capitalized cost to the various project components.

Changes in Estimates

The cost allocations associated with a project are based in part on estimates of costs yet to be incurred. The accountant should review these cost estimates for incomplete projects as part of the closing process in every reporting period. If there is a material change in estimates, this will alter the developer's recognition of costs on a go-forward basis. It does not alter the amounts of costs that have already been recognized in prior periods. This can mean that the profit margins on units sold in the future will differ from the profit margins on units sold in the past, since different costs will be associated with the past and future unit sales.

Changes in Expected Use

When a project is partially complete, it is possible that the developer will alter the use of the real estate in order to produce a higher economic yield. For example, a plan to create a mixed-use strip mall may be replaced by a plan to develop a high-rise condominium complex. Up to this point, all costs incurred have likely been capitalized. What impact does the change in expected use have on these capitalized costs?

The correct treatment is to charge to expense only that portion of these capitalized costs that exceed the estimated completion value of the revised project. There are two additional issues to consider:

- This approach is only possible if there is a formal plan for the developer to switch to the new expected use for the property.
- The costs included in the analysis are those capitalized costs already incurred and to be incurred. The "to be incurred" part of that statement requires estimates of costs not yet incurred, which should be reviewed at regular intervals.

It is possible that a change in use that increases the value of a project also increases the threshold amount of expenses that can be incurred before any losses associated with the project need to be recognized.

Project Abandonment

The circumstances may dictate that a developer abandon a project. For example, a decline in the economy has dried up demand for condominium units, or the developer has lost the financing needed to complete a project. When an abandonment occurs, follow these steps to determine the amount of capitalized cost to charge to expense:

1. Calculate the recoverable amount of the costs. For example, this may be from a sale of the property to a third party.
2. Subtract the recoverable amount from the capitalized amount, and charge the difference to expense in the current period.

If a portion of the capitalized amount is retained because of its recoverable nature, review this amount regularly in future periods to see if it is still recoverable. If not, charge it to expense.

Real Estate Selling Costs

A real estate developer routinely engages in sales and marketing activities during the development and construction work on a project. By doing so, units can be sold as soon as they are ready for use, and advance payments from customers can be used to fund the project. There are several different treatments for these expenditures, as noted in the following sub-sections.

Capitalized Selling Costs

Certain types of selling costs can be capitalized, rather than being charged to expense as incurred. In order to be capitalized, they must meet both of the following conditions:

- There is a reasonable expectation that they will be recovered, either from incidental operations (see the Real Estate Incidental Operations section) or via the sale of the project; and
- The selling costs are being incurred to obtain regulatory approval of the project sales, or because these costs are for tangible assets that are used throughout the selling period to assist in securing the sale of the project.

Examples of the types of selling costs that might be capitalized are:

- Model units (net of the estimated proceeds when they are eventually sold)
- Model furnishings (net of the estimated proceeds when they are eventually sold)
- Sales facilities
- Prospectus legal fees
- Semi-permanent signage

All of the preceding costs can be allocated to individual units, so that they are charged to expense as the related units are sold.

Capitalized Advertising Costs

There are cases when a business engages in direct-response advertising, where the recognition of some costs can be deferred. Examples of costs that may be eligible for deferral are the third-party billings and in-house labor costs associated with idea development, writing ad copy, artwork, printing magazine space, and mailing.

This situation arises when there is a reliable and demonstrated relationship between costs incurred and future benefits achieved. For example, a developer may have a history of obtaining a 1% response rate on all direct mail pieces mailed out. Thus, the cost of obtaining that 1% response rate can be associated with the total cost of the mailing.

Expense recognition for direct-response advertising can be deferred if both of the following conditions are met:

- The advertising is intended to generate sales for which customers can be shown to have responded specifically to the advertising by tracking the names of respondents and the specific advertising that triggered their response, such as a coupon or response card; and
- The advertising results in probable future benefits, which requires persuasive evidence of historical patterns of similar results for the business (historical patterns for the industry as a whole are not allowed). Test market results can be used.

To defer expenses related to direct-response advertising, create a separate cost pool for each significant advertising effort, so that costs can be recognized in direct proportion to the receipt of related customer sales. The costs in each pool are then recognized based on the proportion of actual revenues generated by the campaign to the total revenues expected from the campaign. The estimated amount of total revenues to be received may change over time, which can alter the remaining amortization calculation; prior period results are not altered if there is a subsequent change in the estimated amount of total revenues to be received.

If the carrying amount of advertising costs exceeds the associated amount of remaining net revenues yet to be realized, charge the excess amount of advertising costs to expense in the current period.

There may also be situations where a developer reimburses other parties for some or all of their advertising expenditures related to the real estate sales of the developer. This means that the developer may be recognizing the revenues associated with the advertising reimbursements prior to the reimbursements (since there is a timing delay between when the expenditures are made by other parties and when the company reimburses them). The proper accounting in these situations is to accrue the reimbursements in the periods when the associated revenues are generated.

There may be situations where a developer invests in tangible assets that will be used for multiple advertising campaigns, such as a show booth or a billboard. In these instances, it is acceptable to capitalize the cost of the assets and depreciate them over their expected useful lives.

Selling Costs Charged to Expense

The following costs relate to real estate sale activities, but will probably be charged to expense, based on the preceding criteria for selling costs capitalization:

- Advertising
- Corporate sales department costs
- Grand openings
- Sales brochures
- Sales overhead

Real Estate Rental Costs

Certain types of costs incurred to rent real estate projects can be capitalized, rather than being charged to expense as incurred. In order to be capitalized, they must meet both of the following conditions:

- The costs are related to future rental operations; and
- Their recovery is reasonably expected from future rental operations.

Examples of the types of real estate rental costs that can be capitalized are:

- Grand openings
- Model units
- Model unit furnishings
- Semi-permanent signage
- Rental brochures (unused)

The following costs relate to real estate rental activities, but will probably be charged to expense, based on the preceding criteria:

- Advertising
- Rental overhead

Real Estate Incidental Operations

There may be incidental operations associated with a real estate project. For example, the seller might elect to continue renting space in an office building prior to tearing it down and replacing it with condominiums. The intent is to generate some revenue that can offset the costs of developing or holding the property.

When there is revenue from these incidental operations, the proper accounting is to first net the revenue against any related costs. Further actions are as follows:

1. The excess of any revenues over their costs are accounted for as a subtraction from any capitalized project costs.
2. If the costs of these incidental operations exceed their revenues, charge the difference to expense as incurred.

EXAMPLE

Weatherly Investments is in the process of completing an office building. The building will not be substantially complete and ready for occupancy for several more months. In the meantime, Weatherly rents out space in several units on the ground floor that have been completed. Until the facility is substantially complete, the rental income from these ground floor units is treated as income from incidental operations.

Initial Rental Operations

As noted earlier, certain costs can be capitalized up until the point when a project is considered to be substantially completed and available for occupancy. This point is considered to have occurred when tenant improvements have been completed. Under no circumstances is a project considered to still be under development if more than one year has passed since major construction activity stopped. From this point onward, the accounting for the project changes to the following:

- Operating costs are charged to expense as incurred
- Rental revenues are recognized in income
- Depreciation on all capitalized project costs commences
- Capitalized rental costs are amortized

The last bullet point noted that capitalized rental costs are amortized – there are two ways to conduct this amortization, which are:

- If the costs are directly related to the revenue from a specific lease, amortize the costs over the term of that lease.
- If the costs are not directly related to any lease, amortize the costs over the expected benefit period.

It is entirely possible that certain portions of a project will have been completed and are ready for occupancy, while other portions will not be ready until a later date. If so, it is appropriate to treat the completed sections as separate projects. By doing so, the costs associated with the completed sections can now be amortized.

Real Estate Amenities

Amenities are features that improve the perceived attractiveness of a property, such as a swimming pool or a club house. Other amenities may be required by government mandate, such as a water purification facility. In general, the cost of amenities should be allocated among the various land parcels benefiting from the amenities, but only if development of these parcels is considered probable. This general guidance can vary, depending on the intentions of management. There are two alternatives:

- *Sold or transferred in connection with units.* The developer may intend to sell or transfer an amenity in connection with the sale of individual units. If so, any costs that exceed expected proceeds are to be allocated as common costs. This is because the amenity is directly linked to the development and eventual sale of the project. The common costs classification contains those future operating costs that are the responsibility of the developer, until such time as responsibility is shifted to buyers.
- *Sold separately or retained.* The developer may intend to sell an amenity separately from unit sales, or retain the amenity. In either case, designate as common costs any excess of costs over the expected fair value of the amenity as

of its substantial completion date. If the amenity is later sold at an amount that differs from its estimated fair value less accumulated depreciation, this will result in recognition of a gain or loss on the transaction.

During the period before an amenity is ready for its intended use, it may generate operating income or a loss. If so, this amount is added to common costs. Once the amenity is ready for its intended use, this operating income is instead recognized as part of the current operating results of the developer.

Startup Costs

Startup activities are those activities required to organize a new business, open a new facility, introduce a new product, and so forth. These costs differ from the costs incurred to acquire property and develop it. For example, a bank might construct a building to house a new branch office, for which the associated construction costs are capitalized. Once the building has been completed, new employees must be trained in their tasks, banking software is tested, and security systems are reviewed for compliance with established standards. These additional costs are all considered startup costs.

Essentially, the accounting for startup costs is to expense them as incurred.

EXAMPLE

Resorts Management is opening a new subsidiary in Argentina that will build and operate back-country lodges in the country's Patagonia region. The company incurs the following expenses, all of which should be charged to expense as incurred:

Accounting and legal startup costs	Employee training
Depreciation of new equipment	Nonrecurring operating losses
Employee salary-related costs	Recruiting costs

Presentation and Disclosure Topics

The following sub-sections address various reporting issues for entities that develop or hold real estate, and relate to the prior sections in this chapter.

Classifications within the Statement of Cash Flows

There can be some uncertainty regarding how to classify different real estate transactions within the three main classifications used in the statement of cash flows, which are operating activities, investing activities, and financing activities.

Real estate is usually considered a productive asset, so the payment of cash to acquire such an asset would be reported within the investing activities section. However, if real estate is being acquired specifically for the purpose of resale for a profit, then its treatment is similar to inventory, and it should instead be classified within the operating activities section.

Public Company Disclosures

If a company is publicly-held and submitting reports to the Securities and Exchange Commission (SEC), it must comply with Regulation S-X Rule 5-04(c), which mandates that Schedule III – Real Estate and Accumulated Depreciation be filed. This filing is only required in the following situation:

> The schedule… shall be filed for real estate (and the related accumulated depreciation) held by persons a substantial portion of whose business is that of acquiring and holding for investment real estate or interests in real estate, or interests in other persons a substantial portion of whose business is that of acquiring and holding real estate or interests in real estate for investment. Real estate used in the business shall be excluded from the schedule.

Additional notes regarding the preparation of this schedule are:

- Provide totals for all money columns.
- Include in the description column the type of property and its geographical location.
- The Column E information is to be given at the level of each individual investment, except that miscellaneous investments comprising no more than 5% of the total can be aggregated into a "miscellaneous investments" item.
- Add a reconciliation to the report, reconciling changes in the beginning and ending balances, using the following format:

Balance at beginning of period		$ _____
Additions during period:		
Acquisitions through foreclosure	$ _____	
Other acquisitions	_____	
Improvements etc.	_____	
Other (describe)	_____	_____
Deductions during period:		
Cost of real estate sold	$ _____	
Other (describe)	_____	_____
Balance at close of period		$ _____

- Provide a similar reconciliation for accumulated depreciation.
- If there has been a write-down or reserve against a real estate investment, describe the item and the reason for the write-down or reserve.

- Include a note to Column E that states the aggregate cost for the purposes of determining federal income taxes.
- If there is a material amount of intercompany profits stated in the Column E total, state the amount.

Capitalized Interest Disclosures

If a developer has capitalized any of its interest expense, disclose the total amount of interest cost it incurred during the period, as well as the portion of it that has been capitalized.

EXAMPLE

Suture Corporation discloses the following information about the interest cost it has capitalized as part of the construction of a laboratory facility:

> The company incurred interest cost of $800,000 during the year. Of that amount, it charged $650,000 to expense and included the remaining $150,000 in the capitalized cost of its Dumont laboratory facility.

Imputed Interest Disclosures

Any discount or premium related to a note must be stated in the balance sheet as a deduction from or addition to the face amount of a note. The discount or premium is not to be stated as a deferred charge or deferred credit.

In addition, the description of the note in the financial statement disclosures shall include the effective interest rate.

EXAMPLE

Nascent Corporation discloses the following information in its balance sheet about a note receivable from the sale of property:

Note receivable from sale of property:	
Noninterest bearing note due December 31, 20x7	$3,000,000
Less unamortized discount based on imputed interest rate of 7%	450,000
Note receivable less unamortized discount	$2,550,000

Summary

The general intent of the initial accounting for real estate costs is to capitalize costs into a project asset, which is then offset against the revenue to be gained from the sale or rental of the project. It may be necessary to reallocate costs over the course of a project and possibly write off certain costs. Consequently, the accountant must review completion estimates and cost allocations at the end of each reporting period, to see if they are still valid. This review should continue until a project has been substantially completed and is available for sale or rental.

Chapter 3
Purchase of Income-Producing Property

Introduction

The purchase of real estate may involve the acquisition of an income-producing property, such as an apartment complex that is currently receiving monthly rent payments from its tenants. The acquired entity is likely a separate business in its own right, and will continue to be operated as one subsequent to the acquisition transaction being completed. Since this is essentially a joining of business entities, it is called a business combination.

A considerable amount of detailed accounting is required when a business combination takes place. At its least-complex level, the accounting involves the allocation of the purchase price to the acquiree's assets and liabilities, with any overage assigned to a goodwill asset. However, there are a multitude of additional issues that may apply, such as noncontrolling interests, asset purchases, bargain purchases, and more. These topics are addressed in the following sections.

Relevant Accounting Sources

The information stated in this chapter is derived from the following topic in the Accounting Standards Codification:

- Topic 805, *Business Combinations*

Overview of Business Combinations

A business combination has occurred when a group of assets acquired and liabilities assumed constitute a business. A business exists when processes are applied to inputs to create outputs. Examples of inputs are fixed assets, intellectual property, inventory, and employees. An output is considered to have the ability to generate a return to investors. From the perspective of classifying an income-producing property as a business, it uses fixed assets and employees to generate rental income. For example, an existing hotel is a business, since it has a large number of available rooms and a support staff that is used to generate rental income from customers.

A business combination is accounted for using the *acquisition method*. This method requires the following steps:

1. *Identify the acquirer.* The entity that gains control of the acquiree is the acquirer. This is typically the entity that pays assets or incurs liabilities as a result of a transaction, or whose owners receive the largest portion of the voting rights in the combined entity. One of the combining entities must be the acquirer.

2. *Determine the acquisition date.* The acquisition date is when the acquirer gains control of the acquiree, which is typically the closing date.
3. *Recognize and measure all assets acquired and liabilities assumed.* These measurements should be at the fair values of the acquired assets and liabilities as of the acquisition date.
4. *Recognize any noncontrolling interest in the acquiree.* The amount recognized should be the fair value of the noncontrolling interest.
5. *Recognize and measure any goodwill or gain from a bargain purchase.* See the Goodwill or Gain from Bargain Purchase section for a discussion of goodwill and bargain purchases.

EXAMPLE

South Beach Development buys the Havana Hotel and its adjacent parking garage for $12,000,000. The fair values of the components of this property are as follows:

Land	$3,000,000
Hotel building	5,000,000
Parking garage	1,750,000
Tenant relationships	250,000
Total	$10,000,000

There is a shortfall of $2,000,000 between the purchase price and the fair values of the underlying assets. This differential is assigned to the goodwill asset.

There are a number of additional issues that can affect the accounting for a business combination, as outlined below:

- *Contingent consideration.* Some portion of the consideration paid to the owners of the acquiree may be contingent upon future events or circumstances. If an event occurs after the acquisition date that alters the amount of consideration paid, such as meeting a profit or cash flow target, the accounting varies depending on the type of underlying consideration paid, as noted next:
  - o *Asset or liability consideration.* If the consideration paid is with assets or liabilities, remeasure these items at their fair values until such time as the related consideration has been fully resolved, and recognize the related gains or losses in earnings.
  - o *Equity consideration.* If the consideration paid is in equity, do not remeasure the amount of equity paid.

- *Provisional accounting.* If the accounting for a business combination is incomplete at the end of a reporting period, report provisional amounts, and later adjust these amounts to reflect information that existed as of the acquisition date.

- *New information.* If new information becomes available about issues that existed at the acquisition date concerning the acquiree, adjust the recordation of assets and liabilities, as appropriate.

EXAMPLE

American Service acquires the Cavalier Hotel on December 31, 20X3. American hires an independent appraiser to value Cavalier, but does not expect a valuation report for three months. In the meantime, American issues its December 31 financial statements with a provisional fair value of $4,500,000 for the acquisition. Three months later, the appraiser reports a valuation of $4,750,000 as of the acquisition date, based on an unexpectedly high valuation for the building.

In American's March 31 financial statements, it retrospectively adjusts the prior-year information to increase the carrying amount of fixed assets by $250,000, as well as to reduce the amount of goodwill by the same amount.

Any changes to the initial accounting for an acquisition must be offset against the recorded amount of goodwill. These changes to the initial provisional amounts should be recorded retrospectively, as though all accounting for the acquisition had been finalized at the acquisition date.

The measurement period during which the recordation of an acquisition may be adjusted ends as soon as the acquirer receives all remaining information concerning issues existing as of the acquisition date, not to exceed one year from the acquisition date.

The acquirer will probably incur a number of costs related to an acquisition, such as fees for valuations, legal advice, accounting services, and finder's fees. These costs are to be charged to expense as incurred.

Identifiable Assets and Liabilities, and Noncontrolling Interests

It is entirely possible that the acquirer will recognize assets and liabilities that the acquiree had never recorded in its own accounting records. In particular, the acquirer will likely assign value to a variety of intangible assets that the acquiree may have developed internally, and so was constrained by GAAP from recognizing as assets. Examples of intangible assets that could pertain to an income-producing property appear in the following table.

Intangible Assets for Income-Producing Property

Employment contracts	Lease agreements	Tenant relationships
Internet domain names		Trademarks

A lease agreement that is above the prevailing market rate is considered an asset from the perspective of the acquirer, since it will receive cash flows above the market rate in later periods. Conversely, a lease agreement that is below the market rate is considered by the acquirer to be a liability, since it will be forced to accept reduced cash flows for the remaining term of the lease.

A special option only available to private companies is to not recognize separately from goodwill either of the following two types of intangible assets:

- Customer-related intangible assets, unless they are capable of being sold or licensed independently from other assets
- Noncompetition agreements

If a private company elects to not recognize these types of intangible assets, it must amortize goodwill (see the Goodwill Amortization section).

The accounting treatment for special cases related to the recognition of assets and liabilities is as follows:

- *Contingency fair value not determinable.* It is quite common for a contingent asset or liability to not be measurable on the acquisition date, since these items have not yet been resolved. If so, only recognize them if the amount can be reasonably estimated, and events during the measurement period confirm that an asset or liability existed at the acquisition date.
- *Defined benefit pension plan.* If the acquiree sponsored a defined benefit pension plan, the acquirer should recognize an asset or liability that reflects the funding status of that plan.
- *Indemnification clause.* The seller of the acquiree may agree to an indemnification clause in the acquisition agreement, whereby it will indemnify the acquirer for changes in the value of certain assets or liabilities, such as for unusual bad debt losses from receivables in existence at the acquisition date. In these cases, the seller recognizes an indemnification asset when it recognizes a loss on an item to be indemnified; this should be retrospectively applied as of the acquisition date.

Acquired assets and liabilities are supposed to be measured at their fair values as of the acquisition date. Fair value measurement can be quite difficult, and may call for different valuation approaches, as noted below:

- *Alternative use assets.* Even if the acquirer does not intend to apply an asset to its best use (or use the asset at all), the fair value of the asset should still be derived as though it were being applied to its best use.
- *Noncontrolling interest.* The best way to measure the fair value of a noncontrolling interest is based on the market price of the acquiree's stock. However, this information is not available for privately-held companies, so alternative valuation methods are allowed. This valuation may differ from the valuation assigned to the acquirer, since the acquirer also benefits from gaining control over the entity, which results in a control premium.

EXAMPLE

Industrial Designs acquires a plot of land on which is situated a defunct candy cane manufacturing facility. An adjacent plot of land contains a condominium complex. The company checks with the local zoning board, and learns that it could repurpose the land into a residential development. The company should examine this alternative use, including the costs to demolish the structure and prepare the land for residential use, and compare the outcome to the fair value of the existing manufacturing facility. The analysis should indicate the highest and best purpose of the real estate.

A few assets and liabilities that are initially measured as part of an acquisition require special accounting during subsequent periods. These items are:

- *Contingencies*. If an asset or liability was originally recognized as part of an acquisition, derive a systematic and consistently-applied approach to measuring it in future periods.
- *Indemnifications*. Reassess all indemnification assets and the loss items with which they are paired in each subsequent reporting period, and adjust the recorded amounts as necessary until the indemnifications are resolved.
- *Leasehold improvements*. If the acquirer acquires leasehold improvement assets as part of an acquisition, amortize them over the lesser of the useful life of the assets or the remaining reasonably assured lease periods and renewals.

The Securities and Exchange Commission (SEC) does not allow use of the residual method in deriving the value of intangible assets. The residual method is the two-step process of first assigning the purchase price to all identifiable assets, and then allocating the remaining residual amount to other intangible assets. This SEC guidance only applies to publicly-held companies.

Goodwill or Gain from Bargain Purchase

This section addresses the almost inevitable calculation of goodwill that is associated with most acquisitions, given the high prices paid for many income-producing properties. It also addresses the considerably less common recognition of a bargain purchase.

Goodwill Calculation

Goodwill is an intangible asset that represents the future benefits arising from assets acquired in a business combination that are not otherwise identified. Goodwill is a common element in most acquisition transactions, since the owners of acquirees generally do not part with their properties unless they are paid a premium.

The acquirer must recognize goodwill as an asset as of the acquisition date. The goodwill calculation is as follows:

$$\text{Goodwill} = (\text{Consideration paid} + \text{Fair value of noncontrolling interest})$$

$$- (\text{Assets acquired} - \text{Liabilities assumed})$$

If no consideration is transferred in an acquisition transaction, use a valuation method to determine the fair value of the acquirer's interest in the acquiree as a replacement value.

When calculating the total amount of consideration paid as part of the derivation of goodwill, consider the following additional factors:

- *Fair value of assets paid.* When the acquirer transfers its assets to the owners of the acquiree as payment for the acquiree, measure this consideration at its fair value. If there is a difference between the fair value and carrying amount of these assets as of the acquisition date, record a gain or loss in earnings to reflect the difference. However, if these assets are simply being transferred to the acquiree entity (which the acquirer now controls), do not restate these assets to their fair value; this means there is no recognition of a gain or loss.

- *Share-based payment awards.* The acquirer may agree to swap the share-based payment awards granted to employees of the acquiree for payment awards based on the shares of the acquirer. If the acquirer must replace awards made by the acquiree, include the fair value of these awards in the consideration paid by the acquirer, where the portion attributable to pre-acquisition employee service is considered consideration paid for the acquiree. If the acquirer is not obligated to replace these awards but does so anyways, record the cost of the replacement awards as compensation expense.

Bargain Purchase

When an acquirer gains control of an acquiree whose fair value is greater than the consideration paid for it, the acquirer is said to have completed a bargain purchase. A bargain purchase transaction most commonly arises when a business must be sold due to a liquidity crisis, where the short-term nature of the sale tends to result in a less-than-optimum sale price from the perspective of the owners of the acquiree. To account for a bargain purchase, follow these steps:

1. Record all assets and liabilities at their fair values.
2. Reassess whether all assets and liabilities have been recorded.
3. Determine and record the fair value of any contingent consideration to be paid to the owners of the acquiree.
4. Record any remaining difference between these fair values and the consideration paid as a gain in earnings. Record this gain as of the acquisition date.

EXAMPLE

The owners of Foggy Bottom Hotel have to rush the sale of the business in order to obtain funds for estate taxes, and so agree to a below-market sale to Capital Investments for $5,000,000 in cash of a 75% interest in Foggy Bottom. Capital Investments hires a valuation firm to analyze the assets and liabilities of Foggy Bottom, and concludes that the fair value of its net assets is $7,000,000 (of which $8,000,000 is assets and $1,000,000 is liabilities), and the fair value of the 25% of Foggy Bottom still retained by its original owners has a fair value of $1,500,000.

Since the fair value of the net assets of Foggy Bottom exceeds the consideration paid and the fair value of the noncontrolling interest in the company, Capital Investments must recognize a gain in earnings, which is calculated as follows:

$7,000,000 Net assets - $5,000,000 Consideration - $1,500,000 Noncontrolling interest

= $500,000 Gain on bargain purchase

Capital records the transaction with the following entry:

	Debit	Credit
Assets acquired	8,000,000	
Cash		5,000,000
Liabilities assumed		1,000,000
Gain on bargain purchase		500,000
Equity – noncontrolling interest in Foggy Bottom		1,500,000

Purchase of Assets

The purchase of an income-producing property might not be classified as the purchase of a business. If so, the acquirer is instead considered to be buying the assets and liabilities of the property. The accounting for an asset acquisition encompasses the following situations:

- *Cash consideration paid.* When cash is paid for assets, recognize the assets at the amount of cash paid for them.
- *Noncash assets paid.* Measure assets acquired at the fair value of the consideration paid or the fair value of the assets acquired, whichever is more reliably measurable. Do not recognize a gain or loss on an asset acquisition, unless the fair value of any noncash assets used by the acquirer to pay for the assets differs from the carrying amounts of these assets.
- *Cost allocation.* If assets and liabilities are acquired in a group, allocate the cost of the entire group to the individual components of that group based on their relative fair values.

EXAMPLE

Armadillo Industries acquires the production facility of a competitor, which includes production equipment, a manufacturing facility, and the land on which the facility is located. The total purchase price of this group of assets is $800,000. Armadillo allocates the purchase price to the individual assets in the following manner:

Asset	Fair Value	Percent of Total Fair Value		Purchase Price		Cost Allocation
Production equipment	$325,000	35%	×	$800,000	=	$280,000
Manufacturing facility	400,000	43%	×	800,000	=	344,000
Real estate	200,000	22%	×	800,000	=	176,000
	$925,000	100%				$800,000

Amortization of Intangibles

A number of intangible assets may have been recognized as part of a business combination transaction. If so, the acquirer must amortize these assets over their remaining useful lives. The straight-line method is commonly used for the amortization of intangible assets, but an accelerated method could instead be used, if there were a valid argument that the benefits derived from an intangible asset were being used up at an accelerated rate.

The useful life of an intangible asset should be coupled to the period over which it is expected to generate positive cash flows for the acquirer. The amount to be amortized is the book value of the asset, less any residual value. The residual value of most intangible assets is assumed to be zero, unless the acquirer has a commitment from a third party to acquire such an asset at a future date, and the future purchase price can be reasonably determined by reference to an existing market.

Goodwill

Goodwill is a common byproduct of a business combination, where the purchase price paid for the acquiree is higher than the fair values of the identifiable assets acquired. After goodwill has initially been recorded as an asset, do not amortize it. Instead, test it for impairment at the reporting unit level. Impairment exists when the carrying amount of the goodwill is greater than its implied fair value.

A reporting unit is defined as an operating segment or one level below an operating segment. At a more practical level, a reporting unit is a separate business for which the parent compiles financial information, and for which management reviews the results. If several components of an operating segment have similar economic characteristics, they can be combined into a reporting unit. In a smaller business, it is entirely possible that one reporting unit could be an entire operating segment, or even the entire entity.

The examination of goodwill for the possible existence of impairment involves a multi-step process, which is:

1. *Assess qualitative factors.* Review the situation to see if it is necessary to conduct further impairment testing, which is considered to be a likelihood of more than 50% that impairment has occurred, based on an assessment of relevant events and circumstances. Examples of relevant events and circumstances that make it more likely that impairment is present are the deterioration of macroeconomic conditions, increased costs, declining cash flows, possible bankruptcy, a change in management, and a sustained decrease in share price. If impairment appears to be likely, continue with the impairment testing process. The accountant can choose to bypass this step and proceed straight to the next step.

2. *Identify potential impairment.* Compare the fair value of the reporting unit to its carrying amount. If the fair value is greater than the carrying amount of the reporting unit, there is no goodwill impairment, and there is no need to proceed to the next step. If the carrying amount exceeds the fair value of the reporting unit, recognize an impairment loss in the amount of the difference, up to a maximum of the entire carrying amount (i.e., the carrying amount of goodwill can only be reduced to zero). One should consider the income tax effect from any tax deductible goodwill on the carrying amount of the entity (or the reporting unit), if applicable, when measuring the goodwill impairment loss.

These steps are illustrated in the following flowchart.

Goodwill Impairment Decision Steps

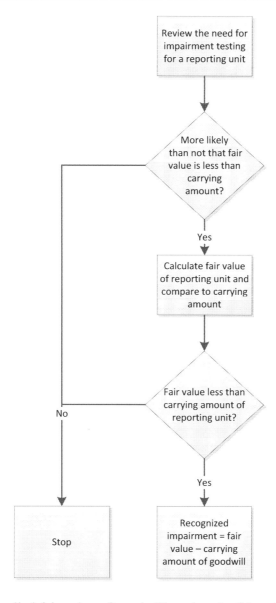

To calculate the implied fair value of goodwill, assign the fair value of the reporting unit with which it is associated to all of the assets and liabilities of that reporting unit. The excess amount (if any) of the fair value of the reporting unit over the amounts assigned to its assets and liabilities is the implied fair value of the associated goodwill. The fair value of the reporting unit is assumed to be the price that the company would receive if it were to sell the unit in an orderly transaction (i.e., not a rushed sale) between market participants. Other alternatives to the quoted market price for a reporting unit may be acceptable, such as a valuation based on multiples of earnings or revenue.

The following additional issues are associated with goodwill impairment testing:

- *Asset and liability assignment.* Assign acquired assets and liabilities to a reporting unit if they relate to the operations of the unit *and* they will be considered in the determination of reporting unit fair value. If these criteria can be met, even corporate-level assets and liabilities can be assigned to a reporting unit. If some assets and liabilities could be assigned to multiple reporting units, assign them in a reasonable manner (such as an allocation based on the relative fair values of the reporting units), consistently applied.
- *Impairment estimation.* If it is probable that there is goodwill impairment and the amount can be reasonably estimated, despite the testing process not being complete when financial statements are issued, recognize the estimated amount of the impairment. The estimate should be adjusted to the final impairment amount in the following reporting period.
- *No reversal.* Once impairment of goodwill has been recorded, it cannot be reversed, even if the condition originally causing the impairment is no longer present.
- *Reporting unit disposal.* If a reporting unit is disposed of, include the goodwill associated with that unit in determining any gain or loss on the transaction.
- *Taxable transaction.* As part of the fair value estimation, determine whether the reporting unit could be bought or sold in a taxable or non-taxable transaction, since this affects its fair value.

Tip: From a practical perspective, it is almost always easier to estimate the fair value of the reporting unit based on a multiple of its earnings or revenues, though this should only be done when there are comparable income-producing properties whose fair values and related multiples are known, and which can therefore be used as the basis for a fair value estimate of the reporting unit.

Impairment testing is to be conducted at annual intervals. The impairment test may be conducted at any time of the year, provided that the test is conducted thereafter at the same time of the year. If the organization is comprised of different reporting units (that is, different income-producing properties), there is no need to test them all at the same time.

Tip: Each reporting unit is probably subject to a certain amount of seasonal activity. If so, select a period when activity levels are at their lowest to conduct impairment testing, so it does not conflict with other activities. Impairment testing should not coincide with the annual audit.

The information used for an impairment test can be quite detailed. To improve the efficiency of the testing process, it is permissible to carry forward this information to the next year, as long as the following criteria have been met:

- There has been no significant change in the assets and liabilities comprising the reporting unit.
- There was a substantial excess of fair value over the carrying amount in the last impairment test.
- The likelihood of the fair value being less than the carrying amount is remote.

Goodwill Amortization

The effort required to monitor the goodwill asset is considered to be excessive for private companies, while the usefulness of goodwill information is also considered to be limited. Consequently, a private company is allowed to amortize goodwill on a straight-line basis over a ten-year useful life. The entity may amortize goodwill over a shorter period if it can demonstrate that a shorter useful life is more appropriate. If an organization chooses to amortize goodwill, it must still test the goodwill asset for impairment at either the entity or reporting unit level. This test is triggered when there is an event that indicates a possible decline in the entity's or reporting unit's fair value to a point below its carrying amount. If an impairment loss is recognized, then any remaining carrying amount is to be amortized over its remaining useful life.

The amortization of goodwill will eventually reduce the carrying amount of an organization's goodwill asset so much that goodwill impairment will be quite unlikely, thereby reducing the need to spend time on such testing.

EXAMPLE

Austin Development discloses the following information about changes in the carrying amount of its goodwill for the year ended December 31, 20X4:

(000s)	Hotel Segment	Apartment Segment	Total
Balance as of January 1, 20X4			
Goodwill	$5,700	$4,200	$9,900
Accumulated impairment losses	-400	-170	-570
	5,300	4,030	9,330
Goodwill acquired during year	360	1,080	1,440
Impairment losses	-250	--	-250
Goodwill written off related to disposal of business unit	--	-200	-200
Balance as of December 31, 20X4			
Goodwill	6,060	5,080	11,140
Accumulated impairment losses	-650	-170	-820
	$5,410	$4,910	$10,320

The company tests the hotel segment in the second quarter of each year. Due to an increase in lower-priced hotels in adjacent locations, management revised its estimate of future cash flows likely to be generated by the hotel segment, and concluded that a goodwill impairment of $250,000 should be recognized. The fair value of the hotel reporting unit was derived using the expected present value of future cash flows.

Presentation and Disclosure Topics

Business combinations are one of the areas in which GAAP requires unusually thorough disclosures. Disclosure topics are addressed under the following headers that describe different aspects of business combinations.

General Disclosures

If an acquirer enters into a business combination during the current reporting period or after the reporting date but before the financial statements are issued or available to be issued, disclose the following information:

- The name of the acquiree and its description
- The acquisition date
- The acquired percentage of voting equity interest in the acquiree
- The reason(s) for the combination
- How the acquirer gained control of the acquiree

If the acquirer is a publicly-held company, disclose the following information:

- The amount of revenue and earnings attributable to the acquiree since the acquisition date and included in the results of the reporting period
- A pro forma statement of the revenue and earnings of the combined entity, as though the acquisition had been completed at the beginning of the year
- If there are comparative financial statements, a pro forma statement of the revenue and earnings of the combined entity, as though the acquisition had been completed at the beginning of all the periods presented
- The nature and amount of any nonrecurring pro forma adjustments attributable to a business combination that are material
- If it is impracticable to report any of the preceding items required for a publicly-held company, disclose why the reporting is impracticable

If the acquirer recognized adjustments in the current reporting period that relate to prior periods, disclose the following information:

- The reason(s) why the initial accounting for a business combination is incomplete
- The specific items for which the accounting is incomplete, including assets, liabilities, equity interests, and/or payments
- The amount and type of any adjustments recognized during the period

The preceding disclosures are still required if a business combination occurs after the reporting date of the financial statements, but before the statements are issued or available to be issued. The only exception is when the initial accounting for the combination is incomplete, in which case one should describe which disclosures were not made, and why they were not made.

Identifiable Assets and Liabilities, and any Noncontrolling Interest

If an acquirer completes a business combination, it should disclose the following information in the period in which the combination was completed:

- *Indemnification assets.* If there are indemnification assets, describe the arrangement, and state the amount recognized as of the acquisition date and the basis for determining it. Also estimate the range of undiscounted outcomes, the reasons why a range cannot be estimated, or if the maximum amount is unlimited.
- *Acquired receivables.* By major class of receivables, state the gross amount and fair value of the receivables, and estimate the contractual cash flow you do not expect to collect.
- *Major asset and liability classes.* State the amount recognized for each major class of assets and liabilities.
- *Contingencies.* State the nature and amount of each asset or liability recognized in relation to a contingency, and how they were measured. You may aggregate disclosures for similar assets and liabilities.
- *Noncontrolling interests.* If the acquirer holds less than 100% ownership of the acquiree, state the fair value of the noncontrolling interest and the valuation method used to arrive at that figure.

If there were several acquisitions in the period that were individually immaterial but material when aggregated, disclose the preceding items in aggregate for the group of acquisitions.

If acquisitions are completed after the balance sheet date but before the financial statements have been issued or are available to be issued, disclose all of the preceding information. However, if the initial accounting for the acquisitions is incomplete, describe the disclosures you were unable to report, and why they could not be made.

Goodwill or Gain from Bargain Purchase

If the acquirer recognizes goodwill as part of an acquisition transaction, disclose the following information for each business combination completed in a reporting period:

- *Bargain purchase.* If the acquisition is a bargain purchase, disclose the resulting gain and the line item in which it is located in the income statement, as well as the reasons why the acquisition generated a gain.
- *Consideration paid.* State the fair value of all consideration paid, as well as by class of asset, liability, and equity item.

- *Contingent assets and liabilities.* In later periods, continue to report any changes in the fair values of unsettled contingent assets and liabilities, as well as changes in (and the reasons for) the range of possible outcomes.
- *Contingent consideration.* If there is consideration contingent upon future events or circumstances, state the amount of this consideration already recognized on the acquisition date, describe the arrangement, estimate the range of undiscounted outcomes or reasons why a range cannot be presented, and whether the maximum payment can be unlimited.
- *Goodwill content.* Describe the factors that comprise goodwill, such as expected synergies from combining the companies.
- *Reconciliation.* Present a reconciliation of the carrying amount of goodwill at the beginning and end of the reporting period.
- *Tax deductibility.* Note the amount of resulting goodwill expected to be tax deductible.

If there were several acquisitions in the period that were individually immaterial but material when aggregated, disclose the preceding items in aggregate for the group of acquisitions.

If acquisitions are completed after the balance sheet date but before the financial statements have been issued or are available to be issued, disclose all of the preceding information. However, if the initial accounting for the acquisitions is incomplete, describe the disclosures you were unable to report, and why they could not be made.

Goodwill Disclosures

A company that has recognized goodwill as an asset should disclose the following information in its financial statements:

- *Estimated impairment.* If a company recognizes an estimated amount of impairment in its financial statements, disclose the fact that the amount recognized is an estimate. In later periods, disclose the nature and amount of any significant adjustments made to the initial estimate.
- *Goodwill carrying amount.* Disclose a reconciliation of changes in the carrying amount of goodwill during the period, showing the beginning gross amount and accumulated impairment losses, additional goodwill recognition, adjustments for deferred tax assets, goodwill related to assets held for sale, impairment losses, other changes, and the ending gross amount and accumulated impairment losses.
- *Goodwill impairment activity.* If there has been goodwill impairment, present the related losses in a separate line item in the income statement, positioned before the subtotal of income from continuing operations.
- *Goodwill impairment loss.* If there is a goodwill impairment loss, disclose the facts and circumstances associated with the loss, the amount of the loss, and how the fair value of the related reporting unit was determined.

- *Goodwill presentation.* State the aggregate amount of goodwill in a separate line item in the balance sheet. If goodwill is being amortized, then this amount should be presented net of the amortization.
- *Unallocated goodwill.* If any goodwill has not been allocated to a reporting unit, disclose the unallocated amount and the reasons why no allocation has been made.
- *Goodwill amortization.* If the organization engages in goodwill amortization, disclose the gross carrying amounts of goodwill, accumulated amortization, and accumulated impairment losses, as well as the aggregate amortization expense for the period.

Summary

An investment entity may acquire a large number of income-producing properties. If so, it is useful to have a standard procedure in place for how to deal with the accounting for these transactions. This can involve setting up a group of business combination experts within the accounting department, perhaps being advised by consultants who have particular expertise in the accounting and tax effects of different variations on business combination accounting.

The testing for goodwill impairment can be both time-consuming and expensive, so consider using the goodwill amortization alternative, which will eliminate this asset from the acquirer's balance sheet within a reasonable period of time, thereby eliminating the need for impairment testing.

Chapter 4
Real Estate Sales

Introduction

The types of sales transactions in the real estate arena are not standardized. There are many ways in which real estate can change hands, including partial sales, exchanges of property, and the sale of time-share intervals. This has led to a wide array of accounting outcomes that do not always reflect the substance of the underlying transactions. A large number of accounting standards have been produced to deal with the situation, which go into great detail regarding the exact criteria needed to have a real estate transaction qualify for a certain type of accounting treatment.

The real estate sales topic is so large that we have divided it into several chapters. This chapter lays out the general revenue recognition alternatives and when they should be used. We then cover more specialized sale topics in three other chapters – Retail Land Sales, Monetary Exchanges, and Time-Sharing Activities.

Relevant Accounting Sources

The information stated in this chapter is derived from the following topics in the Accounting Standards Codification:

- Topic 360, *Property, Plant, and Equipment – General*
- Topic 360, *Property, Plant, and Equipment – Real Estate Sales*
- Topic 606, *Revenue from Contracts with Customers*

Replacement of the Accounting Standards

The current revenue recognition situation is a wide-ranging medley of detailed instructions regarding the treatment of different types of real estate sales. This situation will eventually change, since a new revenue recognition standard has been issued that will supplant the earlier standards. However, there is minimal guidance regarding how the new standard will apply to the recognition of real estate sales. Consequently, we are continuing to present the old cluster of standards in the following sections and chapters. In addition, the new revenue recognition standard is stated in a compressed form in this section.

The new revenue recognition standard establishes a series of actions that an entity takes to determine the amount and timing of revenue to be recognized. The main steps are:

1. Link the contract with a specific customer.
2. Note the performance obligations required by the contract.
3. Determine the price of the underlying transaction.

4. Match this price to the performance obligations through an allocation process.
5. Recognize revenue as the various obligations are fulfilled.

We will expand upon each of these steps in the following sub-sections.

Step One: Link Contract to Customer

The contract is used as a central aspect of revenue recognition. In many instances, revenue is recognized at multiple points in time over the duration of a contract, so linking contracts with revenue recognition provides a reasonable framework for establishing the timing and amounts of revenue recognition.

A contract only exists if there is an agreement between the parties that establishes enforceable rights and obligations. It is not necessary for an agreement to be in writing for it to be considered a contract. More specifically, a contract only exists if the following conditions are present:

- *Approval*. All parties to the contract have approved the document and substantially committed to its contents. The parties can be considered to be committed to a contract despite occasional lapses, such as not enforcing prompt payment or sometimes shipping late.
- *Rights*. The document clearly identifies the rights of the parties.
- *Payment*. The payment terms are clearly stated.
- *Substance*. The agreement has commercial substance; that is, the cash flows of the seller will change as a result of the contract, either in terms of their amount, timing, or risk of receipt.
- *Probability*. It is probable that the organization will collect the amount stated in the contract in exchange for the goods or services that it commits to provide to the other party.

If these criteria are not initially met, the seller can continue to evaluate the situation to see if the criteria are met at a later date.

Step Two: Note Performance Obligations

A performance obligation is essentially the unit of account for the goods or services contractually promised to a customer. The performance obligations in the contract must be clearly identified. This is important when recognizing revenue, since revenue is considered to be recognizable when goods or services are transferred to the customer.

If there is no performance obligation, then there is no revenue to be recognized. If there is more than one good or service to be transferred under the contract terms, only break it out as a separate performance obligation if it is a distinct obligation or there are a series of transfers to the customer of a distinct good or service. In the latter case, a separate performance obligation is assumed if there is a consistent pattern of transfer to the customer.

Step Three: Determine Prices

This step involves the determination of the transaction price built into the contract. The transaction price is the amount of consideration to be paid by the customer in exchange for its receipt of goods or services. The transaction price does not include any amounts collected on behalf of third parties.

The terms of some contracts may result in a price that can vary, depending on the circumstances. For example, there may be discounts, rebates, penalties, or performance bonuses in the contract. Or, the customer may have a reasonable expectation that the seller will offer a price concession, based on the seller's customary business practices, policies, or statements. If so, set the transaction price based on either the most likely amount or the probability-weighted expected value, using whichever method yields that amount of consideration most likely to be paid.

Do not include in the transaction price an estimate of variable consideration if, when the uncertainty associated with the variable amount is settled, it is probable that there will be a significant reversal of cumulative revenue recognized.

If the customer will be paying with some form of noncash consideration, measure the consideration at its fair value. If it is not possible to measure the payment at its fair value, instead use the standalone selling price of the goods or services to be delivered to the customer.

Step Four: Allocate Prices to Obligations

Once the performance obligations and transaction prices associated with a contract have been identified, the next step is to allocate the transaction prices to the obligations. The basic rule is to allocate that price to a performance obligation that best reflects that amount of consideration to which the seller expects to be entitled when it satisfies each performance obligation. To determine this allocation, it is first necessary to estimate the standalone selling price of those distinct goods or services as of the inception date of the contract. If it is not possible to derive a standalone selling price, the seller must estimate it.

There may be a variable amount of consideration associated with a contract. This consideration may apply to the contract as a whole, or to just a portion of it. For example, a bonus payment may be tied to the completion of a specific performance obligation. It is allowable to allocate variable consideration to a specific performance obligation or a distinct good or service within a contract when the variable payment terms are specifically tied to the seller's efforts to satisfy the performance obligation.

There are a number of reasons why the transaction price could change after a contract has begun, such as the resolution of uncertain events that were in need of clarification at the contract inception date. When there is a price change, the amount of the change is to be allocated to the performance obligations on the same basis used for the original price allocation at the inception of the contract.

Step Five: Recognize Revenue

Revenue is to be recognized as goods or services are transferred to the customer. This transference is considered to occur when the customer gains control over the good or service. Construction contracts are likely to be designated as being performance obligations that are transferred over time. Under this approach, they can use the percentage-of-completion method to recognize revenue, rather than the completed contract method. This means that they can recognize revenue as a construction project progresses, rather than waiting until the end of the project to recognize any revenue.

When a performance obligation is being completed over a period of time, the seller recognizes revenue through the application of a progress completion method. The goal of this method is to determine the progress of the seller in achieving complete satisfaction of its performance obligation. This method is to be consistently applied over time, and shall be re-measured at the end of each reporting period.

The preceding discussion was only in a general outline, to show how the revenue recognition process will eventually be implemented. In the following sections, we return to the accounting for real estate sales based on the accounting standards that are currently in effect.

What Constitutes a Real Estate Sale?

A key initial step in applying accounting to the sale of real estate is deciding whether the transaction actually constitutes the sale of real estate. This requires consideration of the entire real estate project component that is being sold. A real estate component involves not only the sale of land, but also of property improvements and any integral equipment (equipment that cannot be readily removed without incurring a significant cost). It is not acceptable to split a transaction into a component involving the sale of land and another component involving the sale of non-real estate, such as buildings and equipment – instead, the real estate designation must be applied to all elements of a transaction.

EXAMPLE

A water park has been sold for $2 million. The pumping facilities are considered to be affixed to the land, since they cannot be removed and used elsewhere without incurring a significant additional expense. This being the case, the entire transaction should be considered the sale of real estate.

Real estate is considered to contain integral equipment when the combined total of the equipment removal cost and the resulting decrease in the fair value of removed equipment is more than 10% of the installed fair value of the equipment. The removal cost is considered to include the estimated cost to ship and reinstall the equipment elsewhere. The fair value of the equipment is assumed to be a sale to a potential buyer that results in the highest possible net cash proceeds.

Eldritch Times has elected to lease property to Upstart Corporation. The property contains a printing press formerly used for the printing of the Eldritch Times newspaper. As of the lease inception date, the fair value of the printing press is $500,000. The estimated cost to remove the equipment is $80,000, which includes a $40,000 repair to the concrete slab on which the press is currently mounted. The estimated cost to ship and install the press at a new site is $32,000, which includes pouring a new concrete slab for the machine.

The total removal cost of the printing press is $120,000, which is 24% of the fair value of the equipment. Since the removal cost is more than 10% of the fair value of the equipment, the cost to remove and use it separately is considered to be significant. Therefore, the printing press is designated as integral equipment.

The sale of timberland or farms is considered to be a sale of real estate, since these sales include land plus the trees or crops that are attached to the land.

Full Accrual Method Revenue Recognition

For sale transactions other than the sale of land (see the Retail Land Sales chapter), there are several types of revenue recognition methods available. The most favorable alternative is the full accrual method, under which the seller can recognize revenue and the associated real estate costs in full (i.e., profit recognition is not deferred). This method is only available when both of the following conditions have been met:

- The collectability of the sales price is reasonably assured or the uncollectible amount can be estimated; and
- The seller does not have to perform any significant activities after the sale.

The collectability of the sales price is supported by evidence that the buyer is making substantial initial and ongoing investments in the property. The buyer should have a sufficiently large stake in the property that there is a large risk of loss from defaulting on any remaining payment obligations. This risk of loss presents an incentive for the buyer to pay its remaining obligations to the seller. Other factors that can be used to assess collectability include:

- The age and location of the property
- The buyer's credit standing
- The cash flows generated by the property

The same criteria apply for profit recognition when the seller sells a partial interest in real estate.

In addition to the conditions just noted, profits can only be recognized under the full accrual method when all of the following criteria have been met:

- A sale transaction has been completed. This is the case when the parties are bound by a contract, all consideration has been exchanged, the seller's involvement in any permanent financing has been completed, and all closing conditions have been completed.
- The initial and ongoing investments by the buyer are adequate, demonstrating a commitment to pay. The adequacy of these investments is discussed in the following sub-section.
- The seller's receivable cannot be subordinated.
- The seller has transferred the risks and rewards of ownership to the buyer, and does not have a substantial continuing involvement in the property.

Buyer's Commitment to Pay

The key element in the preceding profit recognition criteria for the full accrual method is evidence of the buyer's commitment to pay. This topic has received considerable attention in the accounting standards, since many buyers only make a relatively small initial investment.

The adequacy of the initial investment of a buyer is partially based on its size in relation to the sales value of the property. In order to make this calculation, we must first determine the sales value of the property, which requires the following actions:

1. Add to the stated sales price any payments received for an exercised option to buy the real estate, as well as any other fees received that are essentially proceeds from the sale.
2. Subtract from the stated sales price the following items:

    - A discount that reduces the receivable to its present value
    - The net present value of any services to be provided for free
    - The net present value of any services to be provided, in excess of the compensation to be received

The next step is to determine the amount of the buyer's initial investment. This is strictly limited to the following types of payments:

- The down payment
- The buyer's note, backed by an irrevocable letter of credit from an independent bank
- Any payments made by the buyer to other parties to reduce existing property debt
- Other payments by the buyer that are part of the sales value

In this analysis, mortgage insurance cannot take the place of an irrevocable letter of credit. Also, debt incurred by the buyer and secured by the property is not considered part of the initial investment. Further, the following payments are not considered to be part of the buyer's initial investment:

- Buyer payments to third parties to make improvements to the property
- A commitment by a third party to replace the seller's loan with a new loan
- Any funds loaned or refunded to the buyer by the seller
- Any loans guaranteed or collateralized by the seller for the buyer

---

EXAMPLE

A buyer agrees to acquire real estate from Mr. Jones for $250,000, including a cash down payment of $80,000. Mr. Jones plans to loan the buyer $60,000 at a later date. For the purposes of calculating the buyer's initial investment, the future loan of $60,000 is subtracted from the $80,000 cash down payment to arrive at a $20,000 initial investment.

The accounting standards include a table of minimum initial investments that are considered acceptable for using the full accrual method. A buyer must pay at least the amount specified in the following table before the seller can use the full accrual method to recognize revenue.

Table of Minimum Initial Investments

Type of Property	Minimum Initial Investment as Percentage of Sales Value
Land	
Held for commercial, industrial, or residential development that will begin within two years	20
Held for commercial, industrial, or residential development that will begin after two years	25
Commercial and Industrial Property	
Offices and industrial buildings:	
Properties to be leased on long-term basis to entities with satisfactory credit, with cash flow sufficient to service debt	10
Single-tenancy properties sold to a buyer with satisfactory credit	15
All other properties	20
Other income-producing properties:*	
Current cash flow can service debt	15
Deficient cash flow or a start-up scenario	25
Multifamily Residential Property	
Primary residence:	
Current cash flow can service debt	10
Deficient cash flow or a start-up scenario	15
Secondary/recreational residence:	
Current cash flow can service debt	15
Deficient cash flow or a start-up scenario	25
Single Family Residential Property	
Primary residence	5
Secondary/recreational residence	10

* Examples are hotels, marinas, laundries, warehouses, oil wells, manufacturing facilities, power plants, and refineries

If a real estate property is not listed in the preceding table, then use the minimum initial investment percentage for the property type listed in the table that is the most analogous to the property in question, with the most similar risk profile.

If a seller is selling a single-family residential home to a buyer for which it will be the primary residence, and financing is under a Federal Housing Administration or Veterans Administration program, it is acceptable to instead use the normal down payment requirements for those programs, rather than the percentages stated in the preceding table. This is only allowable if the mortgage receivable is fully insured under the applicable program. This approach is used because the mortgage risk has been transferred to the government.

An alternative to using the preceding table exists if the buyer has obtained a loan or firm permanent loan commitment from an independent lender. In this situation, the minimum initial investment is the greater of either of the following options:

- The amount stated in the preceding Table of Minimum Initial Investments; or
- The lesser of 25% of the sales value or the excess of the property's sales value over 115% of the new loan or loan commitment.

EXAMPLE

Evergreen Investments sells a primary residence that has deficient cash flow to service any related debt. According to the table of minimum initial investments, the buyer's initial investment must be at least 15% of the sales value of the property. The sales value of the property is $800,000. The buyer has obtained a firm loan commitment of $560,000 for the property. The minimum amount of the initial investment that the buyer must make so that Evergreen can use the full accrual method is calculated as the greater of the following:

Requirement	Calculation	Amount
Table of minimum initial investments; or	$800,000 × 15%	$120,000
The lesser of:		
Excess of sales value over 115% of loan commitment	$800,000 - ($560,000 × 115%)	156,000
25% of the sales value	$800,000 × 25%	200,000

The calculation reveals that the buyer must make an initial payment of at least $156,000 before Evergreen can use the full accrual method.

The buyer's commitment to pay is no longer an issue when the seller has unconditionally received all amounts related to a sale and is not at risk for any financing related to the sale. For example, the buyer could have paid entirely in cash, or could have assumed the seller's existing nonrecourse debt on the property, or assumed recourse debt with the seller having been released from all debt obligations, or some combination thereof.

The buyer's commitment to pay is also predicated on the adequacy of the buyer's ongoing investment in a property. Such an investment only qualifies for the full accrual method when the buyer is contractually required to make level payments over a period of no more than:

- 20 years if the debt is for land; or
- The customary term of a first mortgage loan by an independent lender for other real estate.

Profit Recognition Not Using the Full Accrual Method

A number of criteria were stated in the last section that limited the situations in which the seller could use the full accrual method. What happens if a transaction does not meet these criteria? There are a number of possible alternative methods available, none of which present as favorable a revenue recognition outcome as the full accrual method. The following sub-sections explain the situations in which certain methods can be used (or not). Since the number of variables results in a highly complex decision tree, we have included at the end of this section a matrix that outlines which method to use, based on a number of initial conditions and sub-conditions. The referenced recognition methods are described later in this chapter.

Sale is Not Completed

If a sale transaction has not been completed, any payments made by the buyer are considered to be a repayment obligation of the seller. As such, the only appropriate accounting approach is the deposit method. This method essentially treats all payments received as a liability, with no sale recognition at all.

There may be situations in which the net carrying amount of a property on the seller's books is greater than the sum of the buyer's deposit, the fair value of any note receivable that has not yet been recorded, and any debt that the buyer will assume once the sale has been completed. In this case, the seller recognizes a loss in the amount of the disparity as soon as the sales agreement is signed. If the buyer instead defaults, or the circumstances indicate that a default will occur, the seller should evaluate whether to recognize an allowance for a loss on the property.

Buyer's Initial Investment Does Not Qualify

The buyer's initial investment in a real estate transaction may not qualify under the preceding criteria that would allow the seller to use the full accrual method to recognize a profit. This presents two alternatives for how to handle the transaction, which are:

- *Cost recovery assured*. If it is reasonably assured that the seller can recover the cost of the property in the event of a buyer default, use the installment method to recognize a profit.
- *Cost recovery not assured*. If it is not reasonably assured that the seller can recover the cost of the property in the event of a buyer default, use the cost recovery method or the deposit method to recognize a profit. The same method usage arises if the seller's cost has already been recovered but there is uncertainty about the recovery of any additional amounts from the buyer.

If the seller is using the installment, cost recovery, or reduced-profit (see the next paragraph) methods to recognize the profit associated with a sale, the seller should not consider as cash payments any debt incurred by the buyer that is secured by the property. However, if the amount of profit deferred is greater than the outstanding amount of seller financing and any property-secured debt for which the seller is contingently liable, the seller can recognize the excess in income.

Buyer's Continuing Investment Does Not Qualify

If the buyer meets the initial investment test but fails the continuing investment test, the seller must use the reduced-profit method at the time of sale to recognize profits. This method is to be used only if the buyer's annual payments will cover the following:

- Both the interest and principal amortization on the maximum first mortgage that could be procured for the property; and
- Interest on the excess of the actual debt on the property over the amount of the maximum first mortgage, using an appropriate interest rate.

If a transaction fails the preceding criteria for the buyer's annual payments, the seller must recognize profits using the installment method or the cost recovery method.

Receivable is Subject to Future Subordination

If the seller's note receivable from the buyer is subject to future subordination, the seller must recognize profits on the transaction using the cost recovery method.

Continuing Seller Involvement

A common situation, especially with commercial properties, is that the seller continues to have some involvement with a property after the sale transaction, and so may not transfer all of the risks and rewards of ownership to the buyer. If so, the profit recognition method to be used depends on the circumstances. The alternatives are:

- *Loss limitation.* If the seller's risk of loss from continuing involvement is limited by the terms of the contract, then the seller can recognize profits at the time of sale, reduced by the maximum loss exposure.
- *Repurchase obligation.* If the terms of the sale agreement could require the seller to repurchase the property, the transaction is not to be considered a sale at all, but rather a financing, leasing, or profit-sharing arrangement. If the seller has an option to buy back property in the event of buyer noncompliance with certain conditions in the sales contract, but the probability of buyer noncompliance is remote, then it is allowable to recognize a sale.
- *Partnership condition.* The seller may be a general partner in a limited partnership that buys some or all of a property, and holds a significant receivable from the buyer for part of the sales price. This situation is accounted for by the seller as a financing, leasing, or profit-sharing arrangement. The receivable is considered to be significant if it is for more than 15% of the maximum first-lien financing that could be obtained from an independent lender.
- *Seller guarantee.* The seller may issue a guarantee to the buyer to either return the buyer's investment or ensure a certain return on investment. If this

guarantee is for an extended period, the seller accounts for the sale as a financing, leasing, or profit-sharing arrangement. If the guarantee only covers a limited period, the seller accounts for the sale using the deposit method until such time as ongoing property operations cover all operating expenses, contractual payments, and debt service; at that point, profits are recognized based on the services performed.

- *Seller operational support.* As part of a sale transaction, the seller may be required to support the operations of a property or operate it at the seller's own risk. If the operational support is for an extended period, the seller accounts for the sale as a financing, leasing, or profit-sharing arrangement. If the operational support is only for a limited period, the seller recognizes profit on the sale based on the services performed. The measurement of services performed is based on the costs incurred and projected to be incurred during the performance period. The seller can begin to recognize profits when there is a reasonable assurance of future rent receipts covering operating expenses and any debt service. When assessing the adequacy of future rent receipts to justify profit recognition, reduce total estimated future receipts by one-third, unless the resulting amount is less than the rents scheduled to be received from signed leases (in which case the rents from signed leases can be used instead).
- *Buyer option to purchase.* A buyer may have only purchased an option to acquire a property. If so, the seller accounts for the payment as a deposit, and only recognizes a profit when the option expires or is exercised.
- *Partial sale.* A seller may only sell a partial interest in a property. In this case, the profit on the transaction is considered to be the difference between the sales value and the proportionate cost of the interest that was sold. The seller can recognize this profit if the buyer is independent from the seller, collection is reasonably assured, and the seller will not have to support the property at a level beyond its proportionate interest. The following accounting applies if these conditions are not present:
  - *No independence.* If the buyer is not independent from the seller, the seller cannot recognize a profit until the partial sale is fully realized through a further sale to an independent third party.
  - *Collection not assured.* If collection of the sales price is not reasonably assured, the seller uses the cost recovery or installment method to recognize a profit.
  - *Excess property support.* If the seller has to subsequently support the property at a level beyond its proportionate interest, profit recognition is based on the nature and extent of the ongoing support obligation.

- *Condominium sales.* When individual units are being sold in a condominium project, the seller recognizes profits using the percentage-of-completion method, but only if all of the following criteria are met. If they cannot be met, the seller uses the deposit method instead. The criteria are:
  - o *Construction is past the preliminary stage.* This means that design work, the execution of construction contracts, site clearance, excavation, and foundations are complete.
  - o *The buyer is committed.* This means the buyer cannot request a refund, other than due to nondelivery.
  - o *Sufficient units have been sold.* The number of units already sold is sufficient to ensure that the property will not revert to a rental property.
  - o *Sales prices are collectible from buyers.* This includes an evaluation of the adequacy of the buyer's initial and continuing investments in the property. This criterion can be addressed by requiring additional and/or larger initial payments from buyers.
  - o *Sales proceeds and costs can be reasonably estimated.* This may involve such considerations as sales price trends, unit demand, and the geographical location.

- *Combined property improvements and land lease.* The seller may sell property improvements to the buyer, while leasing the underlying land. If so, it is not possible to separate the profits on the improvements from the profits on the lease. Instead, the seller should account for the entire transaction as a lease if the lease term is not for a substantial period or does not cover substantially all of the economic life of the property improvements. If this is not the case, the seller instead recognizes a profit on the sale of improvements that is based on the present value of the rental payments not exceeding the seller's land cost, plus the sales value of the improvements, minus the carrying value of the improvements and the land.

EXAMPLE

Lincoln Investments has leased land to the buyer of a new multifamily residential property, and has also sold improvements to the buyer. Key information is a follows:

Sales price of property improvements	$500,000
Improvements paid for as follows:	
Cash down payment	92,000
Bank loan (30-year term at 8%, payable in equal monthly installments	408,000
Total of payments	$500,000
Land lease for 40 years at $9,000 per year, payable monthly in advance	
Cost of improvements is $300,000	
There is no continuing involvement by Lincoln Investments	
Calculation of sales value:	
Present value of 360* monthly land lease payments of $750/month, discounted at 8%	$102,213
Bank loan	408,000
Total debt or equivalent	$510,213
+ Down payment	92,000
Sales value	$602,213

* In the calculation of sales value, the monthly lease payments are limited to 360, to match the term of the bank loan.

The minimum initial investment for a new multi-family residential property is 15%, if Lincoln wants to recognize the sale using the full accrual method. 15% of the $602,213 sales value of the property is $90,332. Since the buyer's deposit is $92,000, the transaction passes the initial investment test.

The sales price of the property improvements is $500,000, while the cost of those improvements is $300,000, leaving $200,000 of profit that can be recognized when the sale is consummated.

- *Future development by seller.* The seller may commit to develop land after the sale of the land to the buyer. This is particularly the case if the buyer can defer payments if the additional development is not completed. If future development costs can be reasonably estimated as of the sale date, the seller can allocate the profit on the sale to the initial sale of the land and to the development thereafter, using the same profit percentage for each activity. The profit related to development is accounted for using the percentage-of-completion method. The seller cannot recognize any profit at the time of sale if it cannot reasonably estimate future development costs.

- *Seller participates in future profits.* The sales agreement may specify that the seller will participate in future profits from a property, and without risk of loss. If so, the seller recognizes the future profits when they are realized.

Decision Tree for Use of Methods

We have outlined a number of revenue recognition methods in this section. Which method should the seller use? The following points can assist in clarifying the situation:

Initial condition	Sub-condition 1	Sub-condition 2	Sub-condition 3	Method to Use
Sale not yet consummated	No further conditions	No further conditions	No further conditions	Deposit method
Sale has been consummated	Initial buyer investment not adequate	Cost recovery not assured	No further conditions	Deposit method or cost recovery method
Same as above	Same as above	Cost recovery is assured	Risks and rewards not transferred	Multiple options
Same as above	Same as above	Same as above	Risks and rewards are transferred	Installment method or cost recovery method
Same as above	Initial buyer investment is adequate	Continuing buyer investment not adequate	Annual payments not greater than obligations	Installment method or cost recovery method
Same as above	Same as above	Same as above	Annual payments greater than obligations	Reduced-profit method
Same as above	Same as above	Continuing buyer investment adequate	Subject to future subordination	Cost recovery method
Same as above	Same as above	Same as above	Not subject to future subordination and risks/rewards not transferred	Multiple options
Same as above	Same as above	Same as above	Not subject to future subordination and risks/rewards transferred	Full accrual method

The situation is even more complex than the preceding matrix indicates. In a few cases in the "method to use" column, even the lengthy list of conditions and sub-conditions was not sufficient to clarify which method should be employed. A further perusal of the preceding discussions is needed in these cases to determine which recognition method to use.

Revenue and Profit Recognition Methods

The following sub-sections describe the recognition methods that can be associated with the sale of real estate, including usage examples.

Installment Method

The installment method is used when the full accrual method is not an option, and the following conditions exist:

- The carrying amount of the property has already been recovered; or
- The recovery of the carrying amount is reasonably assured in the event of a buyer default.

Under the installment method, the seller recognizes a sale, which also means that the real estate asset is removed from the seller's books, along with any debt assumed by the buyer. Profits are initially deferred, and then recognized as the seller receives cash payments from the buyer. Each cash receipt for a principal payment is apportioned between the cost recovered and profit. Interest income is recognized in full when cash is received; it is not accrued. The apportionment uses the ratio of total cost and profit to the sales value of the property.

> **Note:** If the seller grants the buyer a below-market interest rate on a note, this has the effect of reducing the seller's ability to recognize a profit during the early years of a loan. The reason is that interest is normally recognized in full under the installment method when cash is received, while principal payments are partially deferred because they are apportioned between the cost recovered and profit. Thus, if the interest paid is reduced due to a low interest rate, a reduced portion of each payment received can be recognized at once.

Several points regarding the use of this method are:

- Do not reduce the receivable to its present value if the stated interest rate is less than or equal to an appropriate rate. Not using present value will reduce the recognized profit in the earlier years of a transaction.
- The amount of the receivable minus profits not yet recognized cannot exceed the value of the property if it had not been sold.
- If the seller initially adopts the installment method and later meets the requirements for the full accrual method, and the sale is not for retail land, then the seller can switch to the full accrual method, recognizing all remaining profit at that time.

EXAMPLE

Evans Development sells a property to a buyer. Information about the terms of the sale is as follows:

Cash down payment	$100,000
Second mortgage to be paid by buyer to seller	500,000
Total cash received by seller	$600,000
First mortgage assumed by buyer	250,000
Total sales value	$850,000
Seller cost	625,000
Total seller profit	$225,000

The total profit that Evans expects to generate from the transaction is 36% (calculated as $225,000 profit ÷ $625,000).

Following consummation of the sale, the buyer pays $5,000 of principal on the first mortgage and $10,000 of principal on the second mortgage.

The down payment is too small for Evans to use the full accrual method, so it uses the installment method instead. Evans can immediately recognize a profit of $36,000 on the cash down payment (calculated as $100,000 down payment × 36% profit percentage). In addition, Evans can recognize a profit of $5,400 when the two mortgage payments are made (calculated as $15,000 principal paid × 36% profit percentage). The amount of deferred profit remaining to be recognized after the sale date and receipt of the initial mortgage payments is $183,600.

Cost Recovery Method

As was the case with the installment method, the cost recovery method allows for the recognition of a sale, which again means that the real estate asset is removed from the seller's books, along with any debt assumed by the buyer. The cost recovery method mandates that no profit be recognized until the cash payments by the buyer exceed the seller's cost for the property that has been sold. It is therefore a more conservative recognition method than the installment method. This method is most commonly used in situations where recovery of the cost of a property is not reasonably assured if the buyer were to default. Several points regarding the use of this method are:

- The amount of the receivable minus profits not yet recognized cannot exceed the depreciated value of the property if it had not been sold.
- Any gross profit not yet recognized is offset against the receivable on the seller's balance sheet.

- If the seller initially adopts the cost recovery method and later meets the requirements for the full accrual method, then the seller can switch to the full accrual method, recognizing all remaining profit at that time.

EXAMPLE

Edison Properties sells retail store property to Ninja Cutlery for $800,000, for which its own carrying amount is $525,000. Ninja pays for the property as follows:

Cash down payment	$1,000
Note from Ninja	499,000
Mortgage assumed by Ninja	300,000
Sales price	$800,000

The initial investment of $1,000 is far too low to allow Edison to account for the sale using the full accrual method. Also, recovery of the cost is not reasonably assured if Ninja defaults, which eliminates use of the installment method. Instead, Edison must use the cost recovery method.

Following the sale, Ninja makes a $5,000 principal payment on its note to Edison, and an $8,000 payment on the assumed mortgage. The related interest payments are $1,000 on the note and $2,000 on the mortgage. At this point, Edison cannot recognize a profit, since the payments made to date are much less than its $525,000 carrying amount.

The journal entry as of the sale consummation is:

	Debit	Credit
Cash	1,000	
Mortgage	300,000	
Note from buyer	499,000	
Retail store property		525,000
Deferred profit		275,000

The journal entry when the initial loan payments are received (effects of principal and interest are recorded separately) is:

	Debit	Credit
Cash	5,000	
Note from buyer		5,000
Cash	1,000	
Deferred profit		1,000

The payments on the assumed debt are not recorded on Edison's books, since those payments are made to a third party.

Reduced-Profit Method

The reduced-profit method is used when the buyer's initial investment is large enough to qualify for use of the full accrual method, but the buyer's continuing investment does not meet the criteria for the full accrual method. To use this method, the buyer's continuing payments must cover both the interest and principal amortization on the maximum obtainable first mortgage loan on the property, and the interest on any ex-cess debt in excess of the maximum first mortgage loan. If the continuing payments do not meet this minimum payment threshold, then the seller should instead use the installment method or cost recovery method.

The reduced-profit method requires the seller to discount the receivable from the buyer to arrive at the present value of the lowest level of annual payments allowed by the sales contract over the maximum period (capped at 20 years for the sale of land), and excluding any lump sum payment requirements. This is a very conservative profit recognition method, since it only recognizes profits over the longest possible period. Several points regarding the use of this method are:

- When deriving the present value of the receivable, use an appropriate interest rate that is not less than the rate stated in the sales contract.
- Profit recognition of lump sum payments is postponed until these payments actually occur.

The following example illustrates this more complicated recognition method.

EXAMPLE

Monroe Properties sells land for $500,000. The sale transaction involves the use of the following financing arrangements:

Down payment	$150,000
First mortgage – from an independent lender at 8% interest, payable over 15 years, at $35,049 per year.	300,000
Second mortgage – payable to Monroe at 10% interest, payable over 25 years, at $5,508 per year.	50,000
Total price	$500,000

The land originally cost Monroe $300,000, so there is an inherent profit in the sale transaction of $200,000. The market interest rate is 12%

Monroe elects to use the reduced-profit method to recognize the revenue and profits associated with the transaction. The amortization term of the second mortgage is five years longer than the maximum amount allowed for the sale of land.

The recognition of profit is based on the following calculations:

- The present value of the $5,508 second mortgage payment over the maximum period of 20 years at the market interest rate of 12% is $41,142.
- The profit that can be recognized on the sale date is reduced by the difference between Monroe's $50,000 receivable and its reduced present value of $41,142, which is a variance of $8,858.
- The profit recognized on the sale date is the $500,000 sale price minus the $300,000 cost, minus the preceding variance of $8,858, which is a profit of $191,142.
- The remaining $8,858 can be recognized as the related second mortgage payments are received in the 21st through 25th years.

Percentage-of-Completion Method

The percentage-of-completion method is used when the term of a construction contract is relatively long, and the seller wants to recognize a portion of the revenue and profit as the project progresses. Under this method, gross profits are recognized in relation to the proportion of actual-to-expected costs already incurred. The amount of revenue reported is the sum of the project costs incurred in that period and the amount of the recognized gross profit.

EXAMPLE

Hudson Construction is constructing an office building. The expected cost of the project is $10,000,000. At the beginning of Year 1, Hudson sells the property to Apollo Investments for $12,000,000. Apollo is contractually obligated to make payments to Hudson based on the percentage of completion of the project. Hudson expects to generate a profit of $2,000,000 from the project, which is 20% of the expected project costs.

In the first quarter of Year 1, Hudson incurs costs of $3,700,000. The profit calculation for this period is calculated as follows:

$$\frac{\$3,700,000 \text{ Costs incurred}}{\$10,000,000 \text{ Estimated total project costs}} \times \$2,000,000 \text{ Expected profit} = \$740,000 \text{ Profit}$$

Deposit Method

The deposit method requires the seller to not record any profit or note receivable. Any cash received from the buyer is reported as a deposit liability. This is a transitional recognition method that is then replaced by one of the other recognition methods once a sale has been consummated. Several points regarding the use of this method are:

- The seller continues to report the property on its balance sheet, as well as any existing related debt, even if the buyer has assumed the debt. The accompanying disclosures should state that the property is subject to a sales contract.
- The seller continues to recognize depreciation expense on the property, unless the property has been classified as held for sale (see the Real Estate Held for Sale section).
- Any interest received from the buyer that can be refunded is included in the deposit account. Once the sale transaction is completed, this interest is considered part of the buyer's initial investment. However, if any cash received is contractually designated as interest and is not subject to refund, it can be recognized as income, but only to the extent that it offsets carrying charges on the property (such as interest on existing debt or property taxes).
- If a sales contract is cancelled and there is no refund, the amount in the deposit account is recognized as income.

EXAMPLE

Cannabis Central buys a warehouse from Universal Storage in the Denver area, to be used to grow marijuana plants indoors. The contractual price of the transaction is $1,000,000. The components of the payment are as follows:

Cash down payment	$1
Note to Universal Storage	799,999
Nonrecourse mortgage assumed by Cannabis Central	200,000
Total	$1,000,000

The initial down payment is so minor that Cannabis has clearly not demonstrated an initial commitment to pay, so Universal uses the deposit method of accounting to record the transaction, leaving the property on its books. The initial journal entry is:

	Debit	Credit
Cash	1	
Deposit		1

Shortly after the sales contract is signed, Cannabis makes a $10,000 principal payment, along with $3,000 of interest, on the nonrecourse mortgage that it has assumed. The interest payment is nonrefundable. Universal has retained the mortgage on its books, so the entry is:

	Debit	Credit
Mortgage loan	10,000	
Interest expense	3,000	
Deposit		13,000

Cannabis also makes a $20,000 payment to Universal on the $799,999 note, which is divided into $16,000 of principal and $4,000 of interest. This payment is nonrefundable. Universal's entry is:

	Debit	Credit
Cash	20,000	
Deposit		20,000

If Universal has ongoing carrying charges associated with the warehouse, it can recognize the $4,000 interest portion of this second payment as income to the extent that it offsets the carrying charges.

Financing Method

The substance of a sale transaction may indicate that a sale has not actually occurred. Instead, the seller may receive a loan from the buyer that is secured by the property. For example, a seller may accept a loan from a buyer in exchange for a commitment to buy back the property at a later date. In this case, the property remains on the books of the seller, along with any debt obligations that the seller owes to a lender. In addition, the seller records a loan liability in the amount of any cash received from the buyer.

The seller can apply its own incremental borrowing rate to the amount of this obligation. Alternatively, if the seller has committed to buy back the property at a later date, the difference between the original sale price and the buy-back price is considered to be the interest paid on the transaction.

The circumstances of the arrangement may later change sufficiently to allow for treatment as a sale.

EXAMPLE

Bellicose Corporation sells a residential complex to Welton Partners for $15,000,000, and commits to buy back the property in one year for $15,500,000. This is in substance a financing transaction, rather than a sale. Bellicose should record the Welton payment as a loan. The $500,000 difference between the sale and repurchase prices is the interest that Bellicose will pay.

Leasing Method

The preceding finance method was used when a property was to be repurchased at a higher price than its initial sale price. The lease method is used when the repurchase price is *lower* than the original sale price. As was the case with the financing method, the property remains on the books of the seller, along with any debt obligations that the seller owes to a lender. The buyer is considered to be leasing the property from the seller until the buy-back date.

The difference between the original sale price and the buy-back price is treated as rent paid by the buyer. Thus, any cash received from the buyer is accounted for as prepaid rent, which is recognized into income on a straight-line basis over the presumed rental period.

EXAMPLE

Bingo Corporation sells an office building to Willow Partners for $15,000,000, and agrees to repurchase the building in four years for $13,000,000. Bingo records the $2,000,000 difference between the two prices as a prepaid rent liability, and records it as income over the four-year period on a straight-line basis, so that $500,000 is recognized as rental income in each of the four years.

Profit-Sharing Method

The seller of a property may enter into an arrangement where it participates in the profits of the property after it has been taken over by the buyer. If this arrangement does not qualify for accounting as a sale, it is possible that the appropriate treatment is for the seller to keep the property on its books, and to continue to record the operational income and expenses of the property. Since the seller has received a payment from the buyer, the seller records it as a profit-sharing obligation. The exact nature of the accounting will vary, depending on the rights and obligations taken on by the two parties.

Real Estate Project Recoverability

When a real estate project is substantially complete and to be sold or rented, or is being held for development, it is necessary to periodically test it for an impairment loss. If an impairment loss is found, recognize the amount of the impairment at once. Impairment losses cannot be reversed.

An impairment loss on a real estate project should be recognized if its carrying amount is not recoverable and exceeds its fair value. This loss is recognized within the income from continuing operations section of the income statement.

The carrying amount of a project is not recoverable if it exceeds the sum of the undiscounted cash flows expected to result from the sale of a project or its use over its remaining useful life and the final disposition of the asset. These cash flow estimates should incorporate assumptions that are reasonable in relation to the assumptions the entity uses for its budgets, forecasts, and so forth. If there are a range of possible cash flow outcomes, consider using a probability-weighted cash flow analysis.

Impairment testing should be conducted for individual projects that are relatively homogeneous, integral parts of a larger project. This could mean, for example, testing at the level of individual houses, condominiums, and subdivision lots.

EXAMPLE

Albatross Investments is constructing a mixed-use development that includes a condominium tower and a tract of single-family homes. The condominiums and homes would be considered separate groups to be reviewed for recoverability, since the condominiums and homes are considered to be separate, homogenous elements of the project.

Only test for the recoverability of a property whenever the circumstances indicate that its carrying amount may not be recoverable. Examples of such situations are:

- *Cash flow.* There are historical and projected operating or cash flow losses associated with the project.
- *Costs.* There are excessive costs incurred to acquire or construct the project.
- *Disposal.* The project is more than 50% likely to be sold or otherwise disposed of significantly before the end of its previously estimated useful life.

- *Legal.* There is a significant adverse change in legal factors or the business climate that could affect the project's value.
- *Market price.* There is a significant decrease in the project's market price. Alternatively, there is insufficient demand by renters for a rental project.
- *Usage.* There is a significant adverse change in the project's manner of use, or in its physical condition.

If there is an impairment at the level of an asset group, allocate the impairment among the assets in the group on a pro rata basis, based on the carrying amounts of the assets in the group. However, the impairment loss cannot reduce the carrying amount of an asset below its fair value.

Derecognition of Real Estate Project Costs

The sale or rental of a real estate project removes a number of project costs from the books of the developer, since all costs should be recognized at this point and matched with the revenues associated with the sale or rental. The removal of these costs from the records of the developer is known as *derecognition.* The same process occurs under other circumstances, such as when a sales contract is cancelled. The derecognition activities are as follows:

- *Selling costs when project is sold.* If any selling costs related to the project had previously been capitalized, charge them to expense in the period when the offsetting revenue is recognized.
- *Selling costs when contract is cancelled.* When a sales contract associated with a contract is cancelled or the linked receivable is written off, charge all related and unrecoverable selling costs to expense in the same period.
- *Unrecoverable rental costs.* When it appears probable that a lease will be terminated, charge the estimated amount of unrecoverable capitalized rental costs to expense.

A real estate project may also be abandoned. For example, a developer may allow a purchase option to lapse, or simply walks away from a development project. In these situations, all capitalized costs related to such a project should be expensed at once. These costs should *not* be transferred to other parts of the same project if those other parts have not been abandoned, nor should they be assigned to other projects.

Real Estate Held-for-Sale

The held-for-sale asset classification is applied to real estate when the property is ready to be sold. When real estate has been assigned to this classification, the assets are presented separately on the balance sheet of the seller, and they are not depreciated. Real estate can only be classified as held for sale if all of the following criteria are met:

- Management commits to a plan to sell the asset.
- The asset is available for sale immediately in its present condition.
- There is an active program to sell the asset.
- It is unlikely that the plan to sell the asset will be changed or withdrawn.
- Sale of the asset is likely to occur, and should be completed within one year.
- The asset is being marketed at a price that is considered reasonable in comparison to its current fair value.

EXAMPLE

Ambivalence Corporation plans to sell its existing headquarters facility and build a new corporate headquarters building. It will remain in its existing quarters until the new facility is complete, and will transfer ownership of the building to a buyer only after it has moved out. Since the company's continuing presence in the existing building means that it cannot be available for sale immediately, the situation fails the held-for-sale criteria, and Ambivalence should not reclassify its existing headquarters building as held-for-sale. This would be the case even if Ambivalence had a firm purchase commitment to buy the building, since the actual transfer of ownership will still be delayed.

The one-year limitation noted in the preceding criteria can be circumvented in any of the following situations:

- *Expected conditions imposed.* An entity other than the buyer is likely to impose conditions that will extend the sale period beyond one year, and the seller cannot respond to those conditions until after it receives a firm purchase commitment, and it expects that commitment within one year.

EXAMPLE

Ambivalence Corporation has a geothermal electricity-generating plant on the site of its Brew Master production facility. It plans to sell the geothermal plant to a local electric utility. The sale is subject to the approval of the state regulatory commission, which will likely require more than one year to issue its opinion. Ambivalence cannot begin to obtain the commission's approval until after it has obtained a firm purchase commitment from the local utility, but expects to receive the commitment within one year. The situation meets the criteria for maintaining an asset in the held-for-sale classification for more than one year.

- *Unexpected conditions imposed.* The seller obtains a firm purchase commitment, but the buyer or others then impose conditions on the sale that are not expected, and the seller is responding to these conditions, and the seller expects a favorable resolution of the conditions.

EXAMPLE

Ambivalence Corporation enters into a firm purchase commitment to sell its potions plant, but the buyer's inspection team finds that some potions have leaked into the local water table. The buyer demands that Ambivalence mitigate this environmental damage before the sale is concluded, which will require more than one year to complete. Ambivalence initiates these activities, and expects to mitigate the damage. The situation meets the criteria for maintaining an asset in the held-for-sale classification for more than one year.

- *Unlikely circumstances.* An unlikely situation arises that delays the sale, and the seller is responding to the change in circumstances, and is continuing to market the asset at a price that is reasonable in relation to its current fair value.

EXAMPLE

Ambivalence Corporation is attempting to sell its charm bracelet manufacturing plant, but market conditions deteriorate, and it is unable to sell the plant at the price point that it wants. Management believes that the market will rebound, so it leaves the same price in place, even though the market price is probably 20% lower. Given that the price now exceeds the current fair value of the manufacturing plant, the company is no longer marketing it at a reasonable price, and so should no longer list the asset in the held-for-sale classification.

If real estate is classified as held-for-sale, measure the property at the lower of its carrying amount or its fair value minus any cost to sell. If it is necessary to write down the carrying amount of property to its fair value minus any cost to sell, then recognize a loss in the amount of the write down. The seller may also recognize a gain on an increase in the fair value minus any cost to sell, but only up to the amount of any cumulative losses previously recognized.

Presentation and Disclosure Topics

When an entity is using the installment method to record payments from a buyer, it should disclose the following information, either in the income statement or the accompanying notes:

- Sales value
- Gross profit not yet recognized
- Total cost of the sale

When an entity is using the cost recovery method to record payments from a buyer, it should disclose the following information, either in the income statement or the accompanying notes:

- Sales value
- Gross profit not yet recognized
- Total cost of the sale

Also, the unrecognized amount of gross profit is offset against the remaining receivable on the balance sheet.

When an entity is using the deposit method to record payments from a buyer, it should disclose the following information:

- The amount of any nonrecourse debt that has been assumed by the buyer
- The amount of any principal payments by the buyer on assumed mortgage debt

Summary

A central issue for anyone dealing with real estate accounting is when to recognize the revenue and profit associated with the sale of property. The rules for choosing the correct method require a detailed knowledge of the exact terms of each sale transaction. To ensure that the correct method is used, it is helpful to under are met as part of the terms of each sales contract. Otherwise, a seller of multiple properties might find itself having to use many different recognition methods, which results in excessively complex accounting.

Chapter 5
Retail Land Sales

Introduction

Retail land sales involve the sale of land to retail customers. These types of sales typically arise when a business buys a large tract of land, subdivides it into lots, and provides improvements and amenities in order to improve the sales value of the lots. The organization then uses pervasive sales and marketing campaigns to sell the lots to retail customers. The financing of these sales usually involves a minor down payment, with the business providing the remaining financing. Thus, the general environment for retail land sales is the use of large amounts of leverage with little collateral, since the unimproved land has little inherent value.

Relevant Accounting Sources

The information stated in this chapter is derived from the following topic in the Accounting Standards Codification:

- Topic 976, *Real Estate – Retail Land*

Retail Land

In this section, we address the accounting issues related to the sale of lots that have been subdivided from larger tracts of land, and specifically those with the following characteristics:

- *Down payment.* The down payment amount is so small that a bank would not issue a loan for the balance at market rates.
- *Note or contract for remaining balance.* The seller is not able to enforce the terms of the note or contract.
- *Cancellation.* The seller must refund the down payment if the buyer cancels within a predetermined cancellation period.
- *Default.* If the buyer defaults, the seller recovers the land and retains at least some of the principal payments already made.

The following accounting guidance does not relate to the sale of homes, lots to builders, options to purchase real estate, or ownership interests in entities with real estate holdings.

As noted in the introduction, these characteristics most commonly apply to sales of relatively undeveloped land where the financing is highly leveraged. If a buyer does not want to continue making payments, it is relatively easy to walk away, allowing the seller to take back the property.

Given the large amounts of leverage and small down payments involved, retail land sales can be considered at high risk of default. This situation could lead to sellers recognizing revenue and profit too soon, without giving proper consideration to the potential seller default. Consequently, there are specific rules for when profit can be recognized; if there is even a slight variance from the minimum thresholds for an income recognition method, a seller must use an alternative recognition method that will delay income recognition.

Full Accrual Method

The most favorable income recognition method is the *full accrual method*. Under this method, profits can be recognized in full, but only when the related receivables are collectable and the seller has no significant remaining construction or development obligations. In short, a project must be complete before this method can be used. The following conditions must also have been met:

- Any refund period must have expired.
- Cumulative buyer payments are at least 10% of the contract sales price.
- At least 90% of the contracts in the project that are in force six months after the criteria noted for the following percentage-of-completion method will be collected in full. Further discussion of the collectability of receivables follows this conditions list.
- The receivable from the sale cannot be subordinated to new loans on the property, with some exceptions.
- The seller has no obligation to construct amenities or complete the improvement of lots sold.

When using the full accrual method, the cost of sales should be based on a sales figure that is net of any sales for which there is an expectation of future cancellation. The cost of sales includes the costs of land, improvements, and ongoing carrying costs.

There are very specific guidelines for deciding whether receivables are collectible. The receivables associated with a retail land sale project must meet or exceed these guidelines, or else the full accrual method cannot be used. In brief, the seller must extract a representative sample of receivables from the historical data that reflect the latest available collection data, and which cover an adequate period of time. The receivables in this sample shall be considered uncollectible if they are unpaid as of the end of the sample period, using the delinquency periods stated in the following table.

Delinquency Periods

Percent of Contract Price Paid	Delinquency Period
Less than 25 %	90 days
25% but less than 50%	120 days
50% or more	150 days

Longer delinquency periods than those stated in the table can be used if the seller has recourse to the buyer and the buyer is financially capable of making the payments, or if the seller's recent experience has been better.

If all of the preceding criteria will allow the seller to use the full accrual method, it is then allowable to recognize the revenue associated with the sale. However, the full price is probably payable over a number of years, rather than immediately, so it will be necessary to discount all required payments to their present value. The resulting discounted amount should be one that the seller could sell to a third party as of the contract date, assuming that there is no recourse to the seller. The discounting of future payments brings up the following issues:

- *Comparable discount rate.* The discount rate used to calculate present value should be one that an independent lender would have required for a similar transaction.
- *Minimum discount rate.* The rate used should not be less than the amount stated in the sales contract associated with a sale.

If the seller expects to offer incentives in the future to reduce principal obligations for buyers in exchange for accelerated payments, reduce the amount of profit recognized on the date of sale by the amount of these anticipated discounts.

If the seller allows reductions in the principal balance on an unpaid loan, these amounts are to be charged against income as soon as they are granted to buyers.

A provision should be set up for any receivables that are not expected to be collected in future periods. If a contract is cancelled, any remaining receivable balance on that contract is charged against the provision.

In short, the formula used to calculate the net sales figure that can be recognized at once is:

+	Contract sales prices
-	Discount to present value
-	Estimated uncollectible accounts receivable
-	Expected reductions related to prepayment programs
=	Net sales

EXAMPLE

Fortunate Company is a retail land sales company. It acquires a large ranch property, subdivides it into plots, and begins selling the plots. Its marketing efforts are intensive, resulting in the immediate sale at the beginning of its first year of operations of plots with sales prices totaling $3,000,000. The company receives down payments totaling $300,000, matching the company's 10% down payment policy. The interest rate stated in all sales contracts is 8%. A reasonable estimate of the rate that an independent lender would charge is 11%. All of the contracts mandate 10-year payment terms. The best estimate of bad debts is that 9% of the customers will eventually walk away from their contracts.

Based on the facts, the management of Fortunate has concluded that the company can recognize income using the full accrual method. As part of the income recognition calculation, the controller of Fortunate has compiled the following table, which states the present value of the principal payments that it expects to receive:

Year	Annual Payments	Interest Component	Principal Component	Present Value at 11%
1	$402,380	$216,000	$186,380	$167,909
2	402,380	201,090	201,290	163,367
3	402,380	184,986	217,393	158,958
4	402,380	167,595	234,785	154,653
5	402,380	148,812	253,567	150,492
6	402,380	128,527	273,853	146,402
7	402,380	106,619	295,761	142,468
8	402,380	82,958	319,422	138,597
9	402,380	57,404	344,976	134,851
10	402,380	29,806	372,574	131,220
Totals	$4,023,796	$1,323,796	$2,700,000	$1,488,918

The amount of sales that Fortunate can recognize immediately is calculated as follows:

+	$3,000,000	Contract sales prices
-	243,000	Estimated uncollectible accounts receivable*
-	1,211,082	Discount to present value**
=	**$1,545,918**	**Net sales for immediate recognition**

* Calculated as 9% of the contract sales prices less down payments ($2,700,000 × 9%).

** Calculated as principal component of $2,700,000 minus total present value at 11% of $1,488,918.

Percentage-of-Completion Method

If the seller cannot meet the preceding criteria, its next best choice for income recognition is the *percentage-of-completion method*, where profits are recognized in relation to the proportion of actual-to-expected costs already incurred. To use this method, a transaction must meet *all* of the following criteria:

- Any refund period must have expired.
- Cumulative buyer payments are at least 10% of the contract sales price.
- Any remaining receivables are collectible.
- Preliminary project improvements have been completed, and should be completed on time, as evidenced by such factors as the expenditure of funds, the initiation of improvement work, and the existence of engineering plans.

- There are no indications of significant delaying factors, such as being unable to obtain permits, contractors, or equipment.
- There is a reasonable expectation that the land can be developed as intended and will be useful in that role.

The main differentiating factor between the percentage-of-completion method and the preceding full accrual method is that in this case, the seller still has significant construction obligations.

EXAMPLE

Backwoods Enterprises has purchased land in a remote region of eastern Alaska, which cannot currently be reached by any means other than by airplane. Backwoods has represented to potential buyers that it will build a road into the area. However, the planned path of the road crosses a large area of arctic tundra. Tundra contains a thick layer of ice, which is prone to melting in the summer months, turning any road surface into an impassable bog. Given the difficulty of construction, this project fails the criteria for the percentage-of-completion method.

EXAMPLE

Outdoors Enterprises has purchased a large plot of land in West Virginia, which it plans to market to the buyers of its land parcels as an ideal location for their mountain biking activities. The company has constructed roads around the land, built a complete set of trails, and added parking lots at readily accessible trail locations. This is strong evidence that the company is well into its improvement commitments, which indicates that the percentage-of-completion method could be used.

The amount of revenue recognized under the percentage-of-completion method at the time of sale is measured as the proportion of costs already incurred to the total estimated costs to be incurred (which includes marketing and selling costs related to the project). The total estimated costs to be incurred are based on construction costs in the local area (which could differ markedly from average national or regional costs).

If the seller's performance has not yet been completed, then that proportion of revenues related to future costs should only be recognized when the related future costs are incurred.

EXAMPLE

Crestone Corporation has acquired a ranch in the foothills of the Crestone Mountains. It has built roads and basic infrastructure on the ranch property, but still has a significant commitment to build a golf course on the property. The company signed sales contracts for $5,000,000 as of the beginning of Year 1, for which the contractual interest rate is 8%. A reasonable estimate of the rate that an independent lender would charge is 11%. The required down payment percentage is 10%, so Crestone received $500,000 in down payments. Nine percent of total sales are expected to be uncollectible.

The cost of the golf course is significant in relation to total costs, which means that the percentage-of-completion method is the best accounting method for recognizing income. The controller has compiled the following table, which states the present value of the payments that it expects to receive.

Year	Annual Payments	Interest Component	Principal Component	Present Value at 11%
1	$670,633	$360,000	$310,633	$279,849
2	670,633	335,149	335,483	272,278
3	670,633	308,311	362,322	264,930
4	670,633	279,325	391,308	257,754
5	670,633	248,020	422,612	250,820
6	670,633	214,211	456,421	244,003
7	670,633	177,698	492,935	237,447
8	670,633	138,263	532,370	230,995
9	670,633	95,673	574,959	224,752
10	670,633	49,676	620,956	218,701
Totals	$6,706,327	$2,206,327	$4,500,000	$2,481,529

The controller wants to determine the amount of revenue that must be deferred as of the end of the first year. Pertinent information is as follows:

Total sales contracts signed in first year	$5,000,000
Total applicable costs:	
Land costs related to first-year sales	$300,000
Applicable selling and marketing expenses incurred	400,000
Future improvement costs related to first-year sales	1,050,000
Total applicable costs	$1,750,000
Percentage of completion to-date	60%
Percentage of revenue to be deferred	40%
Calculation of revenue to be deferred:	
Gross sales	$5,000,000
Less: Estimated uncollectible accounts receivable*	-$405,000
Less: Discount to present value**	-2,018,471
Net sales	$2,576,529
× 40% of revenue to be deferred	× 40%
Revenue to be deferred	**$1,030,612**

* Calculated as 9% of the contract sales prices less down payments ($4,500,000 × 9%).

** Calculated as principal component of $4,500,000 minus total present value at 11% of $2,481,529.

The seller should review the total estimated costs to be incurred at least once a year. If a revision is required, recalculate the cumulative costs and profits associated with the sale, which may impact the amount and timing of remaining profits to be recognized. In addition, if the adjusted total estimated cost exceeds the previously-recognized revenue, charge the total anticipated loss to expense if the amount can be reasonably estimated and the loss is probable.

Installment Method

If it is not possible to meet the requirements for the full accrual method or the percentage-of-completion method, the next option is to use the *installment method*. This method is commonly used when it is not possible to reasonably estimate the percentage of outstanding receivables that will be collected.

This method apportions cash received from the buyer between the cost recovered and profit. The apportionment uses the ratio of total cost and profit to the sales value of the property. This method can only be used when *all* of the following criteria have been met:

- Any refund period must have expired.
- Cumulative buyer payments are at least 10% of the contract sales price.
- The seller is financially capable of meeting all representations it has made in the sales contract.

EXAMPLE

Bullfrog Development has acquired a ranch in the Ruby Mountains of Nevada, and has used a well-run sales and marketing campaign to completely sell out all of its land parcels in one day, for $10,000,000. The required down payment is 10%, so Bullfrog has already received $1,000,000. Bullfrog is unable to estimate the buyer default rate that may be experienced over the 10-year period that buyers have in which to make all scheduled payments. The company has no further commitments to the buyers. The cost of sales related to the contracts is $3,000,000, and the selling and marketing costs are $1,000,000.

Since it is not possible to anticipate the default rate, the company elects to use the installment method to recognize income. The calculation of profits to be recognized and deferred is as follows:

Sales	$10,000,000
Total applicable costs:	
Cost of sales	3,000,000
Selling and marketing costs	1,000,000
Profit from retail land sales	$6,000,000
Gross profit percentage	60%
Cash received	$1,000,000
Cash received as percentage of sales	10%
Percent of profit that can be recognized	10%
Amount of profit that can be recognized	$600,000
Amount of profit that must be deferred	$5,400,000

The related journal entries are as follows:

	Debit	Credit
Cash	1,000,000	
Accounts receivable	9,000,000	
Revenues		10,000,000
To record the sales associated with consummation of retail land sale contracts		

	Debit	Credit
Cost of sales	3,000,000	
Inventory		3,000,000
To record the incremental costs of sales associated with consummated retail land sale contracts		

	Debit	Credit
Deferred profit on retail land sales (income statement)	5,400,000	
Deferred profit on retail land sales (contra asset)		5,400,000
To defer profit on those sales for which no cash payments have yet been received		

An entity can change from the installment method to the percentage-of-completion method when all of the conditions for using the percentage-of-completion method have been met. If so, the percentage-of-completion method is applied to the entire project, and is accounted for as a change in accounting estimate. As a result of this change, there will be a credit to income. This credit is a combination of the profit not yet recognized, a discounted liability for any remaining future performance, and the amount of any discount needed to reduce receivables to their present values as of the date of change to the new method.

Deposit Method

If a sales transaction does not meet the criteria for any of the preceding income recognition methods, it must be recorded using the *deposit method*. Under this approach, any payments made by a buyer are considered to be deposits, and so are recorded as liabilities of the seller, rather than sales. Once the threshold criteria for one of the preceding recognition methods are achieved, the seller can begin to recognize the deposits as sales and income. Or, if a sales contract is cancelled and there is no refund, the amount in the deposit account is then recognized as income.

The recognition method to be used may not be entirely clear just by perusing the preceding requirements. The following decision tree clarifies how the correct method can be determined.

Profit Recognition Decision Tree for Retail Land Sales

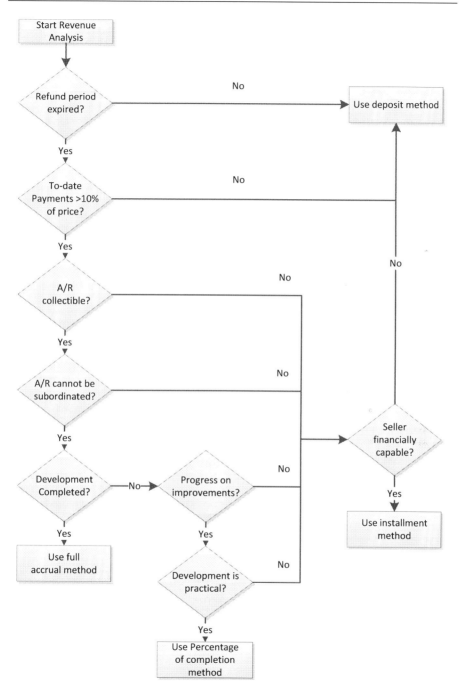

Only one method should be used to recognize the profits from retail land sales within a project. A project for retail land sales is considered to be one within a homogeneous, reasonably contiguous area.

Presentation and Disclosure Topics

When an entity engages in retail land sales, it should disclose the following information:

- The maturities of accounts receivable for each of the next five years
- Accounts receivable that are delinquent, and the method by which delinquency has been determined
- The weighted average interest rate of the receivables, as well as the range of stated interest rates
- The estimated total costs for improvements for major areas from which sales are to be made for each of the next five years, and the estimated dates of these expenditures
- The recorded obligations for improvements to the parcels

If a sale transaction is being accounted for under the deposit method, the seller continues to report the property on its balance sheet, as well as any existing related debt, even if the buyer has assumed the debt. The accompanying disclosures should state that the property is subject to a sales contract.

Summary

The two main factors driving which method to use for income recognition are whether a seller has a remaining commitment to incur costs, and the amount of uncertainty regarding the receipt of any remaining receivables. Both issues may be present in the early stages of a retail land sales project, making it more likely that either the installment sales or deposit methods will be used. As time goes by, the level of uncertainty regarding outstanding receivables tends to decline, since buyers will have invested so much in their land parcels that they are much less likely to default. Consequently, a common accounting scenario is to start using the installment method, and eventually switch to the percentage-of-completion method later in the life of a project.

Chapter 6
Nonmonetary Exchanges

Introduction

Real estate is usually bought and sold in exchange for cash and debt, which makes it relatively easy to determine the prices paid for property. The establishment of a price is necessary for determining the amount of any gain or loss on a transaction. There are times, however, when buyers and sellers exchange real estate, so that there is either no monetary transfer or the monetary portion of a sale is small. In this chapter, we review the accounting for several variations on the concept of the nonmonetary exchange in relation to real estate transactions.

Relevant Accounting Sources

The information stated in this chapter is derived from the following topics in the Accounting Standards Codification:

- Topic 360, *Property, Plant, and Equipment*
- Topic 845, *Nonmonetary Transactions*

Overview of Nonmonetary Transactions

There are several types of nonmonetary transactions, but only one involves exchanges of real estate. This classification is called a *nonmonetary exchange*. The other two types of transactions involve non-cash distributions to either stockholders (such as dividends) or to third parties (such as contributions). The following discussion only involves nonmonetary exchanges.

In general, a reciprocal transfer of a nonmonetary asset is considered an exchange only when each party gives up any continuing involvement in the asset that it has transferred to the other party.

The accounting for a nonmonetary transaction is based on the fair values of the assets transferred. This results in the following set of alternatives for determining the recorded cost of a nonmonetary asset acquired in an exchange, in declining order of preference:

1. At the fair value of the real estate transferred in exchange for it. Record a gain or loss on the exchange.
2. At the fair value of the real estate received, if the fair value of this asset is more evident than the fair value of the real estate transferred in exchange for it.
3. At the recorded amount of the surrendered real estate, if no fair values are determinable or the transaction has no commercial substance.

A transaction is not considered to have commercial substance when an entity's future cash flows are not expected to change to a significant extent as a result of a property exchange. There is presumed to be a significant change in future cash flows under either of the following circumstances:

- The configuration of the before-and-after cash flows has changed significantly. This means the timing, risk, or amount of the cash flows have been altered.
- There is a significant difference between the values of the assets received and transferred, from the perspective of the entity. This is based on the expectations of the receiving and transferring entity regarding how it plans to use an asset.

The cash flows of most real estate properties are unique, so the first criterion for having significantly different cash flows is usually sufficient to qualify a real estate transaction as having commercial substance.

Fair value is considered to be the price that would be received if an asset were sold in an orderly transaction between market participants at the transaction date. It is especially difficult to determine the fair value of raw land, since it does not produce any cash flows that could otherwise be used to derive a discounted cash flow analysis (which can be used as a substitute for fair value).

EXAMPLE

Nascent Corporation exchanges a multi-unit property with a carrying amount of $1,800,000 with Declining Company for a self-storage facility. The multi-unit property had an original cost of $3,000,000, and had incurred $1,200,000 of accumulated depreciation as of the transaction date. No cash is transferred as part of the exchange, and Nascent cannot determine the fair value of the multi-unit property. The fair value of the self-storage facility is $2,000,000.

Nascent can record a gain of $200,000 on the exchange, which is derived from the fair value of the self-storage facility that it acquired, less the carrying amount of the multi-unit property that it gave up. Nascent uses the following journal entry to record the transaction:

	Debit	Credit
Self-storage facility	2,000,000	
Accumulated depreciation	1,200,000	
Multi-unit property		3,000,000
Gain on asset exchange		200,000

EXAMPLE

Nascent Corporation and Starlight Inc. swap warehouses, since the two facilities are in locations that the companies need. The warehouse given up by Nascent has a carrying amount of $2,500,000, which is comprised of an original cost of $4,000,000 and accumulated depreciation of $1,500,000. Both warehouses have identical fair values of $2,700,000.

Nascent's controller tests for commercial substance in the transaction. She finds that there is no difference in the fair values of the properties exchanged, and that Nascent's cash flows will not change significantly as a result of the swap. Thus, she concludes that the transaction has no commercial value, and so should account for it at book value, which means that Nascent cannot recognize a gain of $200,000 on the transaction, which is the difference between the $2,700,000 fair value of the warehouse and the $2,500,000 carrying amount of the warehouse given up. Instead, she uses the following journal entry to record the transaction, which does not contain a gain or loss:

	Debit	Credit
Warehouse (asset received)	2,500,000	
Accumulated depreciation	1,500,000	
Warehouse (asset given up)		4,000,000

Exchanges Involving Monetary Consideration

A common scenario is for one party to a real estate transaction to pay both property and cash (or a note) for the opposing party's real estate. This is done in order to equalize the fair values of the properties being exchanged. In this situation, the transaction must be split into two pieces, which are:

- The portion of the sale involving a monetary payment, which is treated as a sale
- The portion of the sale involving a nonmonetary exchange, which uses the accounting already described for nonmonetary exchanges

The relative fair values of the properties at the date of exchange are used to calculate the amounts of such a transaction that are to be treated as monetary payment or nonmonetary exchange.

If there is a significant amount of monetary consideration paid (known as *boot*), the entire transaction is considered to be a monetary transaction. In GAAP, a significant amount of boot is considered to be 25% of the fair value of an exchange. Conversely, if the amount of boot is less than 25%, the following accounting applies:

- *Payer*. The party paying boot is not allowed to recognize a gain on the transaction (if any).
- *Recipient*. The receiver of the boot recognizes a gain to the extent that the monetary consideration is greater than a proportionate share of the carrying

amount of the surrendered asset. This calculation is based on the percentage of monetary consideration received to either:

- o Total consideration received, or
- o The fair value of the nonmonetary asset received (if more clearly evident)

The recipient's gain calculation is:

$$\frac{\text{Boot}}{\text{Boot} + \text{Fair value of asset received}} \times \text{Total gain} = \text{Gain recognized}$$

If the terms of the transaction indicate that a loss has occurred, the entire amount of the loss is to be recognized at once.

Note: If the boot is at least 25% of the fair value of an exchange of *similar* real estate, the monetary portion of the exchange is treated by the receiver as the sale of an interest in the underlying real estate. See the Real Estate Sales chapter for more information.

EXAMPLE

Nascent Corporation is contemplating the exchange of one of its hotel properties for a museum owned by Aphelion Corporation. The two companies have recorded these assets in their accounting records as follows:

	Nascent (Hotel)	Aphelion (Museum)
Cost	$8,200,000	$9,700,000
Accumulated depreciation	2,200,000	2,700,000
Net book value	$6,000,000	$7,000,000
Fair value	$5,500,000	$7,200,000

Under the terms of the proposed asset exchange, Nascent must pay cash (boot) to Aphelion of $1,700,000. The boot amount is 24 percent of the fair value of the exchange, which is calculated as:

$1,700,000 Boot ÷ ($5,500,000 Fair value of hotel + $1,700,000 Boot) = 24%

Nonmonetary Exchanges

The parties elect to go forward with the exchange. The amount of boot is less than 25 percent of the total fair value of the exchange, so Aphelion should recognize a pro rata portion of the $200,000 gain (calculated as the $7,200,000 total fair value of the property received - $7,000,000 net book value of the property received) on the exchange using the following calculation:

24% Portion of boot to total fair value received × $200,000 Gain = $48,000 Recognized gain

Nascent uses the following journal entry to record the exchange transaction:

	Debit	Credit
Museum (asset received)	7,200,000	
Accumulated depreciation	2,200,000	
Loss on asset exchange	500,000	
Cash		1,700,000
Hotel (asset given up)		8,200,000

Nascent's journal entry includes a $500,000 loss; the loss is essentially the difference between the book value and fair value of the hotel on the transaction date.

Aphelion uses the following journal entry to record the exchange transaction:

	Debit	Credit
Hotel (asset received)	5,348,000	
Accumulated depreciation	2,700,000	
Cash	1,700,000	
Gain on asset exchange		48,000
Museum (asset given up)		9,700,000

Aphelion is not allowed to recognize the full value of the hotel at the acquisition date because of the boot rule for small amounts of cash consideration; this leaves the hotel undervalued by $152,000 (since its fair value is actually $5,500,000).

The accounting is different if the amount of boot is 25 percent or more of the fair value of the exchange. In this situation, both parties should record the transaction at its fair value.

EXAMPLE

Nascent Corporation exchanges an office building for an aquarium owned by Aphelion Corporation. The two companies have recorded these assets in their accounting records as follows:

	Nascent (Office Building)	Aphelion (Aquarium)
Cost	$5,000,000	$9,300,000
Accumulated depreciation	(3,000,000)	(4,000,000)
Net book value	$2,000,000	$5,300,000
Fair value	$2,400,000	$5,800,000

Under the terms of the agreement, Nascent pays $3,400,000 cash (boot) to Aphelion. This boot amount is well in excess of the 25 percent boot level, so both parties can now treat the deal as a monetary transaction.

Nascent uses the following journal entry to record the exchange transaction, which measures the aquarium acquired at the fair value of the office building and cash surrendered:

	Debit	Credit
Aquarium (asset received)	5,800,000	
Accumulated depreciation	3,000,000	
Gain on asset exchange		400,000
Cash		3,400,000
Office building (asset given up)		5,000,000

The gain recorded by Nascent is the difference between the $2,400,000 fair value of the office building surrendered and its $2,000,000 book value.

Aphelion uses the following journal entry to record the exchange transaction, which measures the office building acquired at the fair value of the aquarium surrendered less cash received:

	Debit	Credit
Office building (asset received)	2,400,000	
Accumulated depreciation	4,000,000	
Cash	3,400,000	
Gain on asset exchange		500,000
Aquarium (asset given up)		9,300,000

The gain recorded by Aphelion is the difference between the $5,800,000 fair value of the aquarium surrendered and its $5,300,000 book value.

Exchanges of a Nonfinancial Asset for a Noncontrolling Ownership Interest

There are certain types of nonmonetary exchanges where a business transfers nonfinancial assets to a second entity in exchange for a noncontrolling interest in the second entity. This requires the recognition of the surrendered assets at their fair value (or the fair value of the ownership interest received, if that figure is more readily determinable), and the recognition of a full or partial gain on the transaction.

If the fair value of the assets surrendered exceeds the amount of their carrying value, recognize a gain under either of the following options:

- *Cost method.* If the transferor accounts for the ownership interest received using the cost method, recognize a gain in the full amount of the difference. Under the cost method, an investment is recorded at its historical cost.
- *Equity method.* If the transferor accounts for the ownership interest received using the equity method, recognize a partial gain. In this case, the gain is reduced by the company's portion of its economic interest in the other entity. Under the equity method, the investor records its share of the profits and losses of the investee (see the Real Estate Ventures chapter).

EXAMPLE

Armadillo Industries exchanges property with a carrying value of $1,000,000 and a fair value of $1,500,000 for a 25% economic interest in Armor International. Armadillo accounts for its interest in Armor using the cost method. Armadillo should recognize a gain of $375,000 on the transaction, which is calculated as follows:

$$(\$1,500,000 \text{ Fair value} - \$1,000,000 \text{ Carrying amount}) \times (1 - 25\% \text{ Economic interest}) = \\ \$375,000 \text{ Gain}$$

If the fair value of the assets surrendered is less than the amount of their carrying value, recognize the full amount of the loss at once.

Spin-off Transactions

A business may own several properties, and wants to shift these assets into a different corporate entity. This action may be taken as part of a corporate reorganization, perhaps to more tightly focus different parts of a conglomerate on specific markets. For example, a company might own a number of hotels and shopping malls, and decides to shift these two types of real estate into different entities. It could transfer the assets and operations of the hotels into a new subsidiary, and then distribute shares in the new entity to existing shareholders on a pro rata basis.

In a spin-off transaction, the ownership stays the same, so there is no change in the recorded value of the underlying real estate. A gain or loss can only be recognized if the property is then sold to a third party, at which point the transaction is considered to have commercial substance.

Like-Kind Exchanges

A like-kind exchange occurs when an investment property or business is exchanged for a similar (or like kind) property or business. Internal Revenue Code Section 1031 allows one to avoid recognizing any gain or loss for tax purposes on the exchange transaction. The basic rule of this type of exchange is:

- The assets must be of a similar nature; and
- The owner must use both the original and replacement assets for the same purpose.

In essence, the tax basis of the original property is carried forward into the replacement property. This delays recognition of the associated taxable gain or loss until such time as the replacement property is sold to a third party.

EXAMPLE

Dinwiddie Investments originally acquired a restaurant property for $1,000,000, and has now exchanged it for another restaurant property with a fair value of $1,200,000. The transaction qualifies under IRC Section 1031 as a like-kind exchange. Dinwiddie simply assigns its existing $1,000,000 basis in the original restaurant property to the new property for tax purposes.

In the preceding example, Dinwiddie could continue to exchange restaurant properties many times, and would still be able to use the original $1,000,000 cost basis for all of them, thereby deferring the recognition of any taxable gain or loss.

Note: Properties are considered to be "like-kind" if they are of the same nature. They do not have to be of the same grade or quality.

If a different type of property or a cash payment is made as part of an exchange, then the values of these unrelated items are to be recognized as a taxable gain. However, any portion of the transaction for which there was a like-kind exchange still qualifies under the like-kind exchange rule.

Several other points regarding the like-kind exchange concept are:

- It cannot be applied to an exchange of securities, partnership interests, or inventory.
- It cannot be applied to the exchange of real property where the outgoing property is located within the United States and the replacement property is located outside of the country.

It is allowable to have a deferred exchange of assets that still qualifies as a like-kind exchange. This "Starker" transaction (also known as a 1031 tax deferred exchange) only applies if the replacement property has been identified within 45 days of the asset transfer date and:

- The earlier of the date when the replacement property is received; or
- The due date of the tax return for the tax year in which the transfer initially took place.

During this interim period, a third party retains the cash or other proceeds from the disposition of the first property in an escrow account, and then acquires the replacement property on behalf of the seller and shifts ownership of that property to the seller.

Presentation and Disclosure Topics

If a business engages in nonmonetary transactions, it should disclose the following information:

- *Description*. Disclose the nature of these transactions.
- *Basis*. Describe the basis of accounting for the transferred assets.
- *Gains or losses*. State the amount of any gains or losses recognized in relation to the nonmonetary transfers.
- *Revenue*. State the amount of gross operating revenue resulting from nonmonetary transfers.
- *Transfers*. If inventory is being exchanged, note the related amount of revenues and costs associated with the exchanges at their fair values.

Summary

A nonmonetary exchange of real estate, or one that involves a monetary component, must be examined closely to determine the extent to which a gain (if any) can be recognized. The accounting standards are somewhat conservative in this area, while the Internal Revenue Code is somewhat more liberal in its rules for like-kind exchanges. Consequently, it is entirely possible that a nonmonetary exchange will result in different gain recognition for book and tax purposes.

Chapter 7
Time-Sharing Activities

Introduction

Time-sharing involves selling the right to occupy a property for a certain period of time on a repeating basis. For example, a single condominium unit might have 50 owners, who occupy it for 50 weeks per year, leaving a few weeks for unit maintenance. Buyers must make an initial payment to acquire a slice of occupation time in a unit, and are also assessed a periodic fee, which represents their share of the maintenance and other fees associated with their unit, plus the cost of amenities (such as a swimming pool and golf course).

There are many variations on the basic time-sharing concept, such as exchanges where time-share owners can trade their ownership intervals with the owners of intervals elsewhere in the world, and the use of points-based systems that can be redeemed at different time-share resorts.

The use of time-shares has attracted the attention of the accounting standard-setters to an unusual degree, resulting in the extensive treatment we have outlined in this chapter. The reasons for the outsized accounting requirements for time-shares relates to their risky nature. The payments for time-shares tend to experience high default rates. Also, sellers expend inordinate sums on sales and marketing activities, and may attempt to capitalize these costs in order to avoid recognizing large losses in the early stages of a time-share development. When combined, these issues result in an environment where reported profits by sellers can be unreasonably accelerated, resulting in overblown financial results.

Relevant Accounting Sources

The information stated in this chapter is derived from the following topics in the Accounting Standards Codification:

- Topic 360, *Property, Plant, and Equipment – Real Estate Sales*
- Topic 978, *Real Estate – Time-Sharing Activities*

Time-Share Characteristics

Time-sharing is the conveyance of a right to occupy a dwelling unit during specific future periods. This type of arrangement has the following characteristics:

- Large numbers of homogeneous sales
- Financing by the seller

- High sales and marketing expenditures by the seller
- If there is a buyer default, the seller recovers the time-sharing interval sold to the buyer, and some portion of the buyer's principal paid

In many cases, buyers are able to swap their time-sharing intervals through an exchange, perhaps for a different time period, a different property, or for other types of products. Depending on the type of exchange entity, buyers may have to pay a fee in order to have the right to exchange their time-share intervals.

Criteria for Revenue Recognition

One of the key concerns in time-share accounting is which method the seller is allowed to use to record a sale. There are several possible revenue recognition methods available, depending on the circumstances of a sale. The most favorable method from a profit recognition perspective is the full accrual method, which can only be used when the related receivables are collectable and the seller has no significant remaining construction or development obligations.

Of the two criteria for the use of this method, the one most difficult to determine is the collectability of receivables. The ability of the seller to collect the sales price of a time-share is demonstrated by the buyer's commitment to pay. This commitment to pay concept is supported by evidence of the following:

- A substantial initial investment in the time-share interval
- A substantial continuing investment in the time-share interval

A large early investment by the buyer is considered significant, since it gives the buyer such a large stake in a time-sharing interval that there is a greatly reduced risk of default. Given the importance of the buyer's investment, the following sub-sections address the two types of investment, as well as the related issue of sales value.

Further evidence of collectability includes the credit standing of the buyer, the age and location of the property, and the adequacy of cash flows generated by the property.

Buyer's Initial Investment

We measure the initial commitment to pay by comparing the amount of the buyer's initial investment to the sales value of the interval being purchased. The resulting percentage is then compared to the table of minimum initial investments, which we first introduced in the Real Estate Sales chapter. The table is reproduced here.

Table of Minimum Initial Investments

Type of Property	Minimum Initial Investment as Percentage of Sales Value
Land	
Held for commercial, industrial, or residential development that will begin within two years	20
Held for commercial, industrial, or residential development that will begin after two years	25
Commercial and Industrial Property	
Offices and industrial buildings:	
Properties to be leased on long-term basis to entities with satisfactory credit, with cash flow sufficient to service debt	10
Single-tenancy properties sold to a buyer with satisfactory credit	15
All other properties	20
Other income-producing properties:*	
Current cash flow can service debt	15
Deficient cash flow or a start-up scenario	25
Multifamily Residential Property	
Primary residence:	
Current cash flow can service debt	10
Deficient cash flow or a start-up scenario	15
Secondary/recreational residence:	
Current cash flow can service debt	15
Deficient cash flow or a start-up scenario	25
Single Family Residential Property	
Primary residence	5
Secondary/recreational residence	10

* Examples are hotels, marinas, laundries, warehouses, oil wells, manufacturing facilities, power plants, and refineries

The problem with this table is that time-sharing intervals are not listed. This being the case, we must use the most analogous property type listed in the table, which is the 10% figure used for secondary residences. Thus, evidence of a sufficient initial buyer commitment to pay must be a down payment of at least 10% of sales value.

<u>Impact of Unused Sampler Programs and Mini-Vacations</u>

A buyer may have paid for a sampler program or mini-vacation, and then buys a unit without using up the entire program or vacation. The buyer then applies the unused portion of the sampler or mini-vacation to the sales price. In this case, the unused payment should be considered part of the buyer's initial and continuing investment when determining the buyer's commitment. This is not the case if the buyer has fully used the sampler program or mini-vacation, irrespective of what the sale documents may state.

Buyer's Continuing Investment

To use the full accrual method of accounting, the buyer must also show a substantial continuing investment in a time-share interval. The amount of continuing investment is not considered to be sufficient unless the sales contract requires the buyer to make annual payments on its total debt in an amount at least equaling the level annual payment that would be required to pay the debt and interest over no more than the customary amortization term of a first mortgage loan by an independent lender.

Since the payment term for a typical time-share investment is usually ten years or less, it is relatively easy to meet this criterion.

Sales Value

As noted earlier, the initial and continuing investments of a buyer are judged in relation to the sales value of the time-sharing interval that has been purchased. The calculation of sales value involves the following steps:

1. Add to the stated sales price any payments received for an exercised option to buy the interval, as well as any other fees received that are essentially proceeds from the sale.
2. Subtract from the stated sales price the following items:

   - A discount that reduces the receivable to its present value
   - The net present value of any services to be provided for free
   - The net present value of the fair value of any products or services to be provided, in excess of the compensation to be received
   - The assumed reduction in payments related to prepayment inducements

There are several additional issues related to the sales price that may or may not impact the calculation of sales value. They are as follows:

- *Incentives provided.* Reduce the stated sales price by the amount of any incentives provided. When the incentive is noncash, account for it as a separate deliverable with a related cost of sales. For a cash incentive, account for the amount as a discount from the sales price. A noncash incentive is an incentive that a buyer could elect to purchase, but does not have to purchase (such as an airline ticket voucher). A cash incentive is considered to be either (a) cash or (b) an incentive that the buyer would otherwise have to purchase (such as maintenance fees or closing costs). When an incentive is obtained from an independent third party for cash, the amount paid is likely to be the best estimate of the fair value of the incentive.

EXAMPLE

Lynx Properties sells a time-sharing interval for $80,000. Part of the deal is a voucher that can be used to reduce the price of a cruise by $500. Lynx recognizes revenue from the sale of the interval of $79,500, as well as $500 of revenue from the sale of the $500 voucher. This is considered a non-cash incentive. There will also be a $500 cost of sales associated with the sale of the voucher.

As an alternative, Lynx offers to a different homebuyer a year of free maintenance fees, which would normally be worth $1,000. The sale price for this interval is the same, at $80,000. This is considered a cash incentive. Lynx can recognize revenue from the sale of the interval of $79,000. No other revenue or expense is recognized.

- *Unrelated fees.* The seller may charge a fee that is unrelated to financing, such as a document preparation fee. If so, add this fee to the stated sales price. However, this situation does not apply if the fee is a pass-through fee that is being charged by a third party.

EXAMPLE

Bismarck Properties sells a time-sharing interval for $12,000. Bismarck charges all buyers a flat $100 document preparation fee, irrespective of how they intend to finance the purchase. This changes the sales value to $12,100. If Bismarck had instead been passing through the fee from an independent third-party document preparation firm, there would be no change to the original sales value.

- *Financing fees.* The seller may charge a fee that is related to the financing of a time-sharing interval, such as a loan origination fee. If so, this is to be treated as an adjustment to the interest rate stated on the financing documents.
- *Inducements provided.* When an inducement is provided to a customer, irrespective of whether the individual completes a purchase, the cost of the inducement is treated as a selling and marketing cost that is charged to expense as incurred, rather than an adjustment to the sales price of a time-share interval.

EXAMPLE

Permian Corporation specializes in the construction and sale of time-share intervals. In a recent sale transaction, the stated sales price was $15,000. There was also a $100 document handling fee, which raised the price to $15,100. Against this price was a $250 allowance against the first year of owners' association fees. Permian also offers a $1,000 discount if all payments are made within the first five years of the loan payment period. In addition, the company provides a free $700 airline voucher at closing. Based on this information, the sales value of the interval is calculated as follows:

Stated contract price	$15,000
Add: document handling fee	100
Less: Waived owners' association fee	-250
Less: Early payment incentive	-1,000
Less: Airline voucher	-700
Net sales value	$13,150

Revenue Recognition Methods

The revenue recognition methods applicable to time-share intervals are the same as the methods used for other types of real estate. They are briefly described in this section – see the Real Estate Sales chapter for more detailed explanations, as well as examples.

Full Accrual Method

Under the full accrual method, profits can be recognized in full, but only when the related receivables are collectable and the seller has no significant remaining construction or development obligations. In short, a project must be complete before this method can be used.

Percentage-of-Completion Method

Under the percentage-of-completion method, profits are recognized in relation to the proportion of actual-to-expected costs already incurred (not including selling and marketing costs). This approach is used only when the related receivables are collectable but a time-sharing project has not yet been completed.

Deposit Method

If a sales transaction does not meet the criteria for any of the preceding income recognition methods, it must be recorded using the deposit method. Under this approach, any payments made by a buyer are considered to be deposits, and so are recorded as liabilities of the seller, rather than sales. Once the threshold criteria for one of the preceding recognition methods are achieved, the seller can begin to recognize the deposits as sales and income.

Cost Recognition

The preceding section outlined the methods used to recognize the income related to the sale of time-share intervals. In a normal real estate transaction, one would charge to expense the costs associated with a specific property. This is not possible with time-share transactions, since a large number of interval sales may be associated with a single unit or project. Instead, the cost of sales is based on the pool of costs associated with a project. The calculation used to determine the cost of sales to be associated with a sale transaction is called the *relative sales value method*. In essence, this method determines the cost of sales by applying a cost-of-sales percentage to the total estimated amount of time-sharing revenue. The calculation used for this method is:

$$\text{Period sales} \times \frac{\text{Estimated total project cost}}{\text{Estimated total project sales}} = \text{Period cost of sales}$$

The following issues apply to the use of the relative sales value method:

- *Phase-specific.* The method should be applied separately to each phase of each project.
- *Common costs.* If the seller incurs any common costs, they should be allocated to inventory only among those phases that will be benefited by these costs.
- *Periodic recalculations.* On at least a quarterly basis, a time-sharing seller should recalculate its estimates of total costs and total revenues. The estimate of total revenue is a combination of the actual to-date revenue and expected future revenue, and the determination should include such factors as:
  - Incurred or estimated uncollectibles
  - Changes in sales price or sales mix
  - The repossession of time-share intervals that may be difficult to resell
  - The effects of programs that encourage buyers to upgrade to more expensive intervals
  - The effects of sales incentives to move slower-selling inventory units

  The cost of sales percentage should be recalculated at the same time as total revenues are reviewed. This analysis incorporates the revised total revenue and total cost figures. If the cost of sales must be adjusted, it should be done in the current period.
- *Lower of cost or market.* When there is an inventory of time-share units held for sale, they should be measured at the lower of their carrying amounts or their fair value less costs to sell.
- *Incidental operations.* When a time-share seller is holding an inventory of units, any revenue from renting them and associated rental costs are to be classified as incidental operations. If the amount of incremental revenue

exceeds incremental costs, treat the excess revenue as a reduction of inventory costs. If the amount of incremental revenue is less than incremental costs, charge the excess cost to expense as incurred.

EXAMPLE

Ptarmigan Properties develops and sells time-share intervals. This results in the following sales and collections information:

Unit Type	20X1	20X2	20X3	Total Nbr. of Intervals	Sales Price	Expected Future Revenue
Type A	300	350	150	800	$20,000	$16,000,000
Type B	250	100	100	450	25,000	11,250,000
Type C	100	100	--	200	28,000	5,600,000
	650	550	250	1,450		$32,850,000
Estimated uncollectible notes*						-2,850,000
Estimated future revenue						$30,000,000

* The estimate is rounded to the nearest thousand

Additional information is:

- A down payment of 20% is required for all buyers
- Inventory cost is $9,000,000
- Cost of sales percentage is 30% ($9,000,000 inventory ÷ $30,000,000 estimated revenue)
- Initial estimate of default rate = 8.6758% of expected future revenue

The related accounting entries for 20X1 are as follows:

	Debit	Credit
Notes receivable	$12,040,000	
Cash	3,010,000	
Estimated uncollectible sales	1,305,708	
Sales (20X1)		$15,050,000
Allowance for uncollectible notes receivable		1,305,708

	Debit	Credit
Cost of sales	$4,123,288	
Inventory		$4,123,288

The calculation of the cost of sales noted in the preceding journal entry is as follows:

20X1 Sales	$15,050,000
Less: Estimated uncollectible sales (8.6758%)	-1,305,708
Net sales	$13,744,292
Cost of sales percentage	× 30%
Cost of sales	$4,123,288

The calculation of the remaining inventory at the end of 20X1 is as follows:

Total expected future revenue	$30,000,000
Less: 20X1 net sales	-13,744,292
Remaining expected revenue	$16,255,708
Cost of sales percentage	× 30%
Balance of remaining inventory	$4,876,712

When the 20X1 cost of sales of $4,123,288 is added to the ending inventory of $4,876,712, it equals the $9,000,000 beginning inventory balance.

In 20X2, the same assumptions apply, but Ptarmigan's accountant now drops the 20X1 information from the table, with the following result:

Unit Type	20X1	20X2	20X3	Total Nbr. of Intervals	Sales Price	Expected Future Revenue
Type A		350	150	500	$20,000	$10,000,000
Type B		100	100	200	25,000	5,000,000
Type C		100	--	100	28,000	2,800,000
		550	250	800		$17,800,000
Estimated uncollectible notes*						-1,544,000
Estimated future revenue						$16,256,000

* The estimate is rounded to the nearest thousand

Time-Sharing Activities

The related accounting entries for 20X2 are as follows:

	Debit	Credit
Notes receivable	$9,840,000	
Cash	2,460,000	
Estimated uncollectible sales	1,067,123	
Sales (20X2)		$12,300,000
Allowance for uncollectible notes receivable		1,067,123

	Debit	Credit
Cost of sales	$3,369,863	
Inventory		$3,369,863

The calculation of the cost of sales noted in the preceding 20X2 journal entry is as follows:

20X2 Sales	$12,300,000
Less: Estimated uncollectible sales (8.6758%)	-1,067,123
Net sales	$11,232,877
Cost of sales percentage	× 30%
Cost of sales	$3,369,863

The calculation of the remaining inventory at the end of 20X2 is as follows:

Total expected future revenue	$16,256,000
Less: 20X2 net sales	-11,232,877
Remaining expected revenue	$5,023,123
Cost of sales percentage	× 30%
Balance of remaining inventory	$1,506,937

When the 20X1 and 20X2 cost of sales of $4,123,288 and $3,369,863 are added to the ending inventory of $1,506,937, it equals (with rounding) the $9,000,000 20X1 beginning inventory balance.

Time-Sharing Activities

In 20X3, the same assumptions apply, but Ptarmigan's accountant now drops the 20X2 information from the preceding table, with the following result:

Unit Type	20X1	20X2	20X3	Total Nbr. of Intervals	Sales Price	Expected Future Revenue
Type A			150	150	$20,000	$3,000,000
Type B			100	100	25,000	2,500,000
Type C			--	--	28,000	--
			250	250		$5,500,000
Estimated uncollectible notes*						-477,000
Estimated future revenue						$5,023,000

* The estimate is rounded to the nearest thousand

The related accounting entries for 20X3 are as follows:

	Debit	Credit
Notes receivable	$4,400,000	
Cash	1,100,000	
Estimated uncollectible sales	477,169	
Sales (20X3)		$5,500,000
Allowance for uncollectible notes receivable		477,169

	Debit	Credit
Cost of sales	$1,506,849	
Inventory		$1,506,849

The calculation of the cost of sales noted in the preceding 20X2 journal entry is as follows:

20X3 Sales	$5,500,000
Less: Estimated uncollectible sales (8.6758%)	-477,169
Net sales	$5,022,831
Cost of sales percentage	× 30%
Cost of sales	$1,506,849

The final cost of goods sold calculation has eliminated all remaining inventory.

Additional Time-Share Transactions

The preceding sections have dealt with the essentials of which recognition methods to use, depending on the circumstances of a sale transaction. In addition, there are many other accounting transactions that may arise, such as the proper treatment of selling costs, the accounting for debt restructurings, and the transition of an existing interval to an upgraded interval. These topics and more are addressed in the following sub-sections.

Additional Products and Services

When a buyer is to receive additional products and services as well as a time-sharing interval as part of a sale arrangement, all payments received by the seller should be allocated as though there are two separate notes receivable – one is for the sale of the interval, and the other is for the other products and services. These presumed notes should have the following characteristics:

- They have the same interest rate
- The note related to the interval has a term equal to the term of the note signed by the buyer
- The note related to the other products and services has a term that runs through the date when the buyer can use the items

To establish that future performance by the buyer is sufficient, the contractual principle and interest payments from the buyer needed to receive the incentive must at least equal the fair value of the incentive.

EXAMPLE

Eagle Time Shares sells a time-sharing interval to Mr. Hawk for $50,000. At the time of sale, Eagle receives a $5,000 down payment and will issue a $2,500 incentive to Mr. Hawk that is based on Hawk's future performance. Hawk's monthly payment to Eagle under the terms of the note is $875. If Hawk is required to make a minimum of three monthly payments (totaling $2,625) before being eligible for the incentive, Hawk's initial and continuing investments will not be reduced for the amount of the incentive.

If the future performance of the buyer is not sufficient, the seller must instead reduce its measurement of the buyer's commitment by the amount by which the fair value of the incentive exceeds the amount paid by the buyer for the incentive.

EXAMPLE

The preceding example sale transaction between Eagle Time Shares and Mr. Hawk changes, so that Hawk is only required to make a minimum of **one** monthly payment before being eligible for the $2,500 incentive. In this case, Eagle must reduce the initial $5,000 down payment by the $1,625 difference between the one $875 monthly payment and the $2,500 incentive. This means that Eagle is considered to have received a $3,375 down payment, and the sales value of the time-sharing interval is considered to be $45,000.

When a portion of a buyer's down payment is assumed to apply toward the payment of an incentive, that portion is not considered when calculating the buyer's initial and continuing investments.

Treatment of Selling Costs

Any costs incurred to sell time-sharing intervals should be charged to expense as incurred. Examples of these costs are:

- Costs incurred for failed sale transactions
- Maintenance
- Sales office rent
- Telemarketing call centers
- Telephone expenses
- Utilities

If the seller is incurring costs to bring customers to a tour location, all related costs are charged to expense at the time of the tour.

EXAMPLE

Aggressive Corporation locates a group of 20 people living in Oklahoma, who are interested in seeing Aggressive's time-sharing project in San Diego. The company books flights and hotel reservations for the group in May, at a cost of $5,000. The tour is scheduled for June. Aggressive should record the expenditure as a prepaid expense (asset) in May, and charge it to expense in June.

The only case in which the recognition of selling costs can be deferred is when one of the following two conditions is present:

- The cost can be reasonably expected to be recovered by selling time-share intervals, or by the proceeds from incidental operations; and the cost was incurred to acquire tangible assets that are used in the selling process (such as model units, sales property, and semi-permanent signs) or for services performed in order to obtain regulatory approval of sales (such as the filing of a prospectus).

- The cost can be reasonably expected to be recovered by selling time-share intervals, and it is directly associated with a sale transaction, and the cost would not have been incurred in the absence of a sale transaction (such as a commission).

When selling costs have been deferred, they should be charged to expense in the same period in which the associated profit is to be recognized. When a time-share interval is sold, selling costs are to be allocated to that sale transaction based on the relative fair values of the intervals available for sale within the related project or phase. If there is a sales contract cancellation prior to the recognition of a profit, any related deferred selling costs that are not recoverable are to be charged to expense at once.

If the deposit method is being used to account for sale transactions, the amount of selling costs that can be deferred is limited to the non-refundable portion of the deposit paid by the buyer. This requirement avoids the seller's risk of not being able to recover deferred selling costs if a buyer defaults.

EXAMPLE

Camelot Time-Shares has deferred the recognition of $500 in selling costs. The sales manager expects to close the related time-share contract in May. In late April, she learns that the prospective buyer has just lost all of his investments in a Ponzi scheme, and can no longer commit to the contract. This is a sales contract cancellation, so she must authorize the immediate recognition of the deferred selling costs.

Effects of Below-Market Financing

There may be instances in which the seller provides financing to a time-share buyer at an interest rate that is below the market rate. If so, it is necessary to record the transaction using an interest rate that more closely accords with the market rate. The rate that should be used is one that approximates the rate that would have been used if an independent borrower and lender had entered into a similar arrangement under comparable terms and conditions.

If available, the preferred option for deriving imputed interest is to locate the established exchange price of the goods or services involved in the transaction, and use that as the basis for calculating the interest rate. The exchange price is presumed to be the price paid in a cash purchase, which is its sales value. Any difference between the present value of the note and the sales value shall then be accounted for as a change in interest expense (i.e., as a note discount or premium), which is amortized over the life of the note.

If it is not possible to determine the established exchange price, an applicable interest rate must be derived at the time the note is issued. The rate selected should be the prevailing rate for similar borrowers with similar credit ratings, which may be further adjusted for the following factors:

- The credit standing of the borrower

- Restrictive covenants on the note
- Collateral on the note
- Tax consequences to the buyer and seller
- The rate at which the borrower can obtain similar financing from other sources

Any subsequent changes in the market interest rate shall be ignored for the purposes of this transaction.

Estimating Uncollectible Receivables

In the time-share industry, a substantial proportion of all notes outstanding may not be collectable. This means there is a risk that the amount of profit recognized from time-share sales will be overstated by the amount of bad debt losses. To avoid this overstatement, it is necessary to recognize an estimate of uncollectability as a reduction of revenue when profit is recognized under either the full accrual or percentage-of-completion methods. This uncollectability adjustment also calls for a corresponding adjustment in the cost of sales, and must be conducted on at least a quarterly basis. If the allowance is adjusted as a result of this evaluation, there is a corresponding adjustment to revenue in the current period by altering the contra-revenue account.

To evaluate whether the amount in the allowance for uncollectibles is sufficient, it may be necessary to consider a number of factors, including the following:

- The year in which the unit was sold
- The terms of the contract
- The seller's collection experience with these types of contracts
- The location of the time-share units
- The age of the notes receivable
- General economic conditions

EXAMPLE

Hadrian Properties is selling time-share intervals in the San Diego area. The project is quite similar to another project that Hadrian recently completed in the adjacent community of Chula Vista, which allows the company to use the historical data from the Chula Vista project to estimate the uncollectibles that will arise from the San Diego project. Based on this analysis, Hadrian expects a 15% default rate.

In the current year, 20X4, Hadrian sells $5,000,000 of time-share intervals in its San Diego project. At a 15% expected default rate, Hadrian should expect $750,000 of these sales to eventually default, and so creates a reserve for this amount. During the year, $213,000 of the sales do indeed default, which are offset against the reserve in the current year. This means the remaining balance in the reserve account has declined to $537,000, which reflects the defaults that are expected to occur in later years.

Debt Restructurings

In order to maximize the collection of payments under notes receivable, the sellers of time-shares use a number of collection methods. These methods include the modification of note terms, deferred payments, and downgrades to lower-value time-shares. All of these actions are considered to be forms of troubled debt restructurings.

A change to the terms of a note receivable is considered a debt restructuring. Examples of debt restructurings are payments in the equity of the debtor, reducing the stated interest rate, and reducing the face amount of the debt. In essence, a concession has been granted when the creditor no longer expects to collect all amounts due, and any additional guarantees or collateral received do not offset the amount of the expected loss. When a restructuring results in an insignificant payment delay, this is not considered a concession. The accounting for debt restructurings is as follows:

- *Charge off.* Any reduction in a note receivable due to a note modification is to be charged against the allowance for uncollectibles.
- *Legal fees.* When the creditor incurs legal fees as part of a troubled debt restructuring, charge them to expense as incurred.

If interest income has been accrued and proves to be uncollectible, charge it against interest income as soon as the determination of uncollectability is made.

Deferral of Rental Costs

A time-share seller may rent units in its inventory during a holding period. If so, the costs incurred to rent these units may be deferred if both of the following conditions are present:

- The costs are directly associated with rental units, and where the recovery of these costs is reasonably expected from the rentals; and
- The costs would not have been incurred if the rental transaction had not occurred.

These deferred rental costs are then charged to expense when the related rental activity occurs, or netted to reduce inventory costs.

EXAMPLE

A customer reserves a time-share interval for the following month as a rental unit. The seller receives the referral from a third-party website, which is owed a $25 placement fee. The seller can recognize this fee as a prepaid expense (asset) and charge it to expense in the following month, when the customer pays the rent on the reserved unit.

Upgrade Transactions

An upgrade transaction is one in which a time-share customer transfers from ownership of a lower-priced to a higher-priced time-sharing interval. In this case, the seller shifts the buyer's initial and continuing investments from the original interval to the calculation of the buyer's commitment criteria for the upgraded interval, which may include any additional down payment made on the higher-priced interval. Profit recognition now applies to the sales value of the upgraded interval.

EXAMPLE

Castle Pines Properties sells a time-share interval to Mr. Smith for $20,000. The terms include a 10% down payment, with financing by Castle Pines. The contractual sales price of the transaction equals the sales value of the interval. There are no issues with collection, as Mr. Smith pays a total of $5,000 of principal to Castle Pines over the succeeding two years.

Two years later, Mr. Smith agrees to an upgrade, where he will shift to a corner unit that has a sales value of $30,000. Castle Pines does not require Mr. Smith to make an additional down payment as part of this transaction.

The controller of Castle Pines wants to know if Mr. Smith's investment as of the upgrade is sufficient for it to use the full accrual method for income recognition purposes. The required down payment percentage to use the accrual method is 10% of the upgraded interval's sales value, which is $3,000. As of the date of the upgrade, Mr. Smith has made a total of $7,000 in down payment and principal payments, which easily exceeds the $3,000 minimum threshold.

Reload Transactions

A reload transaction occurs when a customer is given a second time-sharing interval while retaining the right to the first interval. A reload transaction is treated as a separate transaction from the sale of the first time-sharing interval. Since a reload is a separate transaction, do not include the buyer's initial and continuing investments from the first time-sharing interval in the measurement of the buyer's commitment related to the second time-sharing interval.

Payments by Seller to Support Operations

When a seller has just begun to sell time-sharing intervals, there will likely be too few dues payments being received from interval owners for the owners' association to meet its maintenance and other obligations. To avoid losses by the association, the seller may subsidize its operations. These subsidies by the seller are to be charged to expense as incurred. Once the initial sales period has been completed, the seller will likely pay to the association any dues owed on those intervals that the seller still owns. These dues should also be charged to expense as incurred. In some cases, the seller may be contractually entitled to recover from the owners' association some portion of its initial subsidy. If so, the seller can record a receivable for this amount, but only if payment by the owners' association is probable and the amount of the receivable can be reliably measured.

Management Services

The seller of time-share intervals may be hired as the manager of an owners' association. If so, the seller is entitled to a management fee. The seller should only recognize this fee if the amount has been earned and is realizable. If the seller is subsidizing the owners' association, then any fee revenue it receives must be offset against the amount of the subsidy expense.

It is not common for the sellers of time-share intervals to also provide services as part of a sales contract. Instead, a seller typically provides ongoing management services to owners' associations on a cost-plus basis, with fees usually in the range of 5% to 15% of costs incurred.

Operation of Affinity Programs

A developer of time-shares may operate an affinity program or similar arrangement, where the buyers of time-shares can exchange their intervals for other items, such as airline tickets or hotel rooms. Under these programs, the developer can rent out the interval that has been exchanged, and purchases the exchanged services from other parties, such as hotel chains and airlines. The developer may reserve the right to alter the terms of its award program, so that the rental value of the intervals it is receiving can be matched against the cost of the items it must purchase from third parties.

EXAMPLE

Baton Rouge Properties currently offers 2,000 points in its affinity program to the holders of time-share intervals during the second week of March. A major new festival is initiated during this period, resulting in much higher rental rates that can be charged. Consequently, the company offers interval buyers 2,500 points in its affinity program if they are willing to exchange their intervals during the designated week.

Holding Period

A holding period is the time interval during which a time-sharing interval is held for sale. The holding period begins when units are available for sale. During this period, the time-share seller may engage in a variety of marketing programs, such as mini-vacations and sampler programs, in an effort to sell the inventory of time-sharing intervals. In a holding period, the seller should not depreciate the inventory of time-sharing units. If there are rental activities outside of this holding period, the associated units should be depreciated.

Impairment

If a seller of time-sharing intervals recognizes anticipated losses on those intervals, it should also evaluate all unsold time-share intervals for impairment. Under this evaluation, the seller recognizes an impairment loss on an interval if its carrying amount is not recoverable and exceeds its fair value. The amount of an impairment loss is the difference between an interval's carrying amount and its fair value. Once an impairment loss is recognized, this reduces the carrying amount of the interval.

The carrying amount of an interval is not recoverable if it exceeds the sum of the undiscounted cash flows expected to result from the interval. If there are a range of possible cash flow outcomes, consider using a probability-weighted cash flow analysis.

Accounting Changes and Error Corrections

The developer of a time-share project may change the designation of what constitutes the project and its phases. Such a change may relate to alterations in the facts and circumstances relating to the project, such as construction delays, design changes, or a decision to alter the mix of units to be offered. These changes in designation are to be accounted for as a change in accounting estimate, which mandates a current-period adjustment.

However, if there is a change in the project and phase designations without a corresponding (and supporting) change in the facts and circumstances, this is instead considered a change in the method of applying an accounting principle.

Whenever there is a change in accounting principle, retrospective application of the new principle to prior accounting periods is required, unless it is impracticable to do so. If it is impracticable to retroactively apply changes to prior interim periods of the current fiscal year, then the change in accounting principle can only be made as of the start of a subsequent fiscal year.

The activities required for retrospective application are:

1. Alter the carrying amounts of assets and liabilities for the cumulative effect of the change in principle as of the beginning of the first accounting period presented.
2. Adjust the beginning balance of retained earnings to offset the change noted in the first step.
3. Adjust the financial statements for each prior period presented to reflect the impact of the new accounting principle.

If it is impracticable to make these changes, then do so as of the earliest reported periods for which it is practicable to do so. It is considered impracticable to make a retrospective change when any of the following conditions apply:

- *Assumptions.* Making a retrospective application calls for assumptions about what management intended to do in prior periods, and those assumptions cannot be independently substantiated.
- *Efforts made.* The company has made every reasonable effort to do so.
- *Estimates.* Estimates are required, which are impossible to provide due to the lack of information about the circumstances in the earlier periods.

When making prior period adjustments due to a change in accounting principle, do so only for the direct effects of the change. A direct effect is one that is *required* to switch accounting principles.

EXAMPLE

The managers of Epic Properties decide to subdivide a time-sharing project into three additional phases. This decision is made in order to account for the project in a different way – there are no changes in the operational or financial circumstances of the project that support this change. Since there is no change in the nature of the project itself, the alteration should be considered a change in the method of applying an accounting principle.

Special-Purpose Entities

A seller of time-sharing intervals may establish a special-purpose entity (SPE). These SPEs are typically created in order to sell intervals within countries to non-residents, where non-residents are not allowed to own real estate. In essence, buyers acquire shares in the SPE, rather than ownership in a time-sharing interval.

Such an SPE is considered to have no economic substance and to have been established solely to facilitate sales when the following two conditions are present:

- The SPE is legally required to sell time-sharing intervals to nonresident customers; and
- The SPE has no assets, other than the time-sharing intervals, as well as no debt.

If such an interval is present, the seller should state on its balance sheet as time-sharing inventory the interest in the SPE that has not yet been sold to buyers. Also, the seller does not have to consolidate the SPE or use the equity method or cost method to recognize its investment in the SPE (see the Real Estate Ventures chapter).

Assumptions and Sales of Debt

An assumption of a note receivable occurs when one debtor takes over from the original debtor. From a time-sharing perspective, this means that the arrangement with the original time-share buyer is terminated, and is replaced by a new arrangement with a new buyer. There are two accounting actions to take as a result of an assumption, which are:

1. Charge the remaining balance on the original note receivable to the allowance for uncollectibles.
2. Create a new sale transaction with the new buyer.

A time-share seller may sell a group of notes receivable without recourse. In this situation, the buyer of the notes cannot pursue the seller for any subsequent buyer non-payments on the notes. In this transaction, the seller may not be paid the book value of the group of notes. If the difference in selling price is attributable to a change in the market interest rate from the origination date of the notes, then record the gain or loss as an adjustment of interest income. If the difference in selling price is instead attributable to a change in the credit quality of the notes or other factors, then record the gain or loss as an adjustment to revenue.

Leases

One of the tenets of real estate accounting is that a profit can be recognized only when title has been transferred to the buyer. For time-sharing transactions, this requirement can be handled with a contract-for-deed arrangement. This is a purchase contract under which the seller agrees to convey title at some future point, to be triggered by the buyer having paid a certain percentage of the price of a time-sharing interval. However, if title can revert back to the seller, then the transaction is instead considered to be an operating lease.

Presentation and Disclosure Topics

An entity engaged in the sale of time-shares should disclose the following information:

- The policies used to assess buyer commitment and the collectability of receivables
- The maturities of notes receivable for each of the following five years, and in aggregate for all years thereafter, and a reconciliation to the notes receivable figure stated in the balance sheet
- The weighted average and range of interest rates associated with the notes receivable
- The estimated cost to complete any remaining improvements and promised amenities
- A reconciliation of the activity in the allowance for uncollectibles during the reporting period, including beginning and ending balances, additions related to current-period sales, direct write-offs, and changes in estimate. The same reconciliation should be provided for any receivables that have been sold with recourse.

SAMPLE DISCLOSURE

(000s)	12/31/X2	12/31/X1
Due in 1 year	$32,100	$29,400
Due in 2 years	25,700	23,500
Due in 3 years	20,100	18,800
Due in 4 years	16,400	15,100
Due in 5 years	13,100	12,000
Due beyond 5 years	19,700	18,100
Total receivables	$127,100	$116,900
Total receivables per balance sheet	$127,100	$116,900
Weighted average interest rates	10.3%	10.5%
Reconciliation of activity in the allowance for uncollectibles:		
Balance, beginning of year	$7,294	$7,014
Allowance for uncollectibles on current year sales	5,780	5,600
Write offs of uncollectible receivables	-5,605	-5,320
Changes in estimate for prior years' sales	--	--
Balance, end of year	$7,469	$7,294

When a seller is engaged in time-sharing activities, its financial statement presentation should include the following items:

- Present any changes in time-sharing notes receivable in the statement of cash flows as being cash flows from operating activities.
- Include in the balance sheet the gross notes receivable from time-sharing sales, as well as deductions for the allowance for uncollectibles and for any deferred profit.

Summary

The accounting for time-share intervals is among the most complex real estate topics, since it must deal with the effects of high loan default rates and receivables that may be difficult to estimate. Further, this type of sale involves very high selling and marketing expenses, which sellers prefer to defer whenever possible. In addition, the seller will likely have to negotiate with a high proportion of buyers to structure their debt payments, which calls for the use of restructuring entries. And, if the seller is trying to sell time-share intervals in foreign locations, it may even be necessary to use special-purpose entities to meet the requirements of the local government. In short, this is a high-risk sales environment for the seller that can lead to uncertain outcomes, which makes it a challenging environment for the accountant.

Chapter 8
Rent Topics

Introduction

The assumption in most of the other chapters has been that real estate is bought and sold, so most of the accounting has been based on the outright transfer of property. However, there are many situations in which a property owner leases real estate to tenants for fixed periods of time. This chapter addresses a number of accounting issues relating to these rental arrangements.

Relevant Accounting Sources

The information stated in this chapter is derived from the following topics in the Accounting Standards Codification:

- Topic 360, *Property, Plant, and Equipment*
- Topic 840, *Leases*

Types of Leases

A lease is an arrangement where the lessor agrees to allow the lessee to use a property for a stated period of time in exchange for one or more payments. The general types of leasing arrangements are as follows:

- *Gross lease.* This lease states a fixed amount that the tenant will pay through the term of the lease. This amount includes the facility rent and the tenant's share of all operating expenses. Because the lease amount is fixed, the lessor takes on the risk that operating expenses will be higher during the term of a lease. For example, the terms of a gross lease might specify monthly payments of $10,000 in Year 1 and $10,500 in Year 2 – and no other charges.
- *Net lease.* This lease states a fixed base rent, plus the tenant's proportionate share of operating expenses and property taxes. This arrangement shifts the risk of incurring excess operating costs to the tenant. It is also known as a triple net lease. For example, a tenant might pay $50.00 per square foot, plus its 10% pro rata share of a building's operating expenses. See the Operating Expense Issues section for more detail regarding how operating expense billings are calculated.
- *Base-year lease.* This lease states a fixed amount for the first year of a lease that includes both the facility rent and the tenant's share of all operating expenses in that year. In subsequent years, the tenant can be billed for its share of the excess amount by which operating expenses have increased since the base year.

Morrow Associates enters into a $60 per square foot lease for 20,000 square feet of office space in a building owned by Tennant Partners, using a base-year lease agreement. The operating expenses of the building in the first year were $2,000,000, of which Morrow's share was 4%, or $80,000. This amount was built into the base-year lease.

In the following year, the operating expenses of the building increase to $2,100,000. Morrow is responsible for 6% of the $100,000 incremental increase, so Tennant bills it for $6,000 in Year 2, in addition to the Year 2 rent.

Contingent Rent

A lease arrangement may contain a clause that allows the lessor to participate in the sales of a tenant if the tenant's sales exceed a certain threshold amount during a lease period. This arrangement is most common for retail stores, where sales information can be directly tied to a rented space. The lessor should recognize these additional rent payments only if the minimum measurement threshold has been exceeded. However, the tenant should accrue this additional expense as soon as the amount can be estimated and it is probable that the expense will be incurred.

EXAMPLE

Barnaby Properties rents retail space to Yum-Yum Candies. In addition to the normal monthly rent payment, the lease agreement also stipulates that Yum-Yum will pay 3% of its excess sales to Barnaby for any sales exceeding $1,500,000. At the end of the year, the total sales of Yum-Yum were $1,800,000, so it must pay an additional $9,000 to Barnaby (calculated as sales above the threshold of $300,000 × 3%).

Lease Incentives

A lease incentive is either a payment made directly to a lessee or to the benefit of a lessee in exchange for the lessee committing to a property lease. There are many types of lease incentives, such as:

- Buyout of existing lease
- Free rent for a period of time
- Free leasehold improvements
- Free parking
- Reduced rent for a period of time
- Up-front cash payments

If an incentive is included in a lease (such as several months of free or reduced rent), both the lessee and the lessor recognizes the lease incentive on a straight-line basis over the term of the lease. The lessee accounts for it as a reduction in rent expense, while the lessor accounts for it as a reduction in rent income. Thus, most lease incentives are deferred and recognized over time, rather than being recognized in full as incurred.

Leasehold Improvements

Leasehold improvements are defined as the enhancements paid for by a tenant to leased space. Examples of leasehold improvements are:

- Interior walls and ceilings
- Electrical and plumbing additions
- Built-in cabinetry
- Carpeting and tiles

Leasehold improvements generally revert to the ownership of the landlord upon termination of a lease, unless the tenant can remove them without damaging the leased property.

The lessee should capitalize leasehold improvements, and then depreciate them over the shorter of their useful life or the remaining term of the lease. Depreciation should begin as soon as the improvements are substantially complete and the rental space is ready for its intended use.

The remaining lease term for depreciation purposes can be extended into additional lease renewal periods if the renewal is reasonably assured (such as when there is a bargain renewal option). If the lessor subsequently purchases the property, the improvements can then be depreciated over the estimated remaining useful life of the building.

EXAMPLE

Armadillo Industries has a five-year lease on an office building, as well as an option to renew the lease for an additional five years at the then-prevailing market rate. Armadillo pays $150,000 to build offices in the building immediately after it leases the space. The useful life of these offices is 20 years. Since there is no bargain purchase option to renew the lease, it is not reasonably assured that Armadillo will renew the lease. Consequently, the company should depreciate the $150,000 over the five years of the existing lease, which is the shorter of the useful life of the improvements or the lease term. The annual entry to recognize the depreciation is:

	Debit	Credit
Depreciation expense	30,000	
Accumulated depreciation		30,000

Technically, leasehold improvements are amortized, rather than being depreciated. This is because the actual ownership of the improvements is by the lessor, not the lessee. The lessee only has an intangible right to use the asset during the lease term.

Intangible rights are amortized, not depreciated. However, there is no real effect on the income statement of using one term over the other, especially if the amortization and depreciation expenses are combined for presentation purposes.

Prepaid Rent

When a landlord enters into an agreement to rent space to a tenant, a common provision of the rental agreement is that the tenant will pay the landlord at the beginning of the month. This payment is associated with the month at the beginning of which it is paid. The landlord typically records these payments as rental income in the month in which the cash is received.

But what if the tenant were to pay slightly earlier, at the end of the preceding month? In this case, the landlord must record the receipt of cash, but cannot yet record rental income, since it has not yet earned the rent. Earning the rent will occur in the next month, which is the period to which the payment applies. Instead, the landlord records unearned rent.

To account for this unearned rent, the landlord records a debit to the cash account and an offsetting credit to the unearned rent account (which is a liability account). In the month of cash receipt, the transaction does not appear on the landlord's income statement at all, but rather in the balance sheet (as a cash asset and an unearned income liability).

In the following month, the landlord earns the rent, and now records a debit to the liability account to clear out the liability, and a credit to the revenue account to recognize the revenue. The impact of the transaction now appears in the income statement, as revenue.

What is the accounting by the tenant for this situation? An early payment by the tenant would normally appear in its income statement as rent expense in the period in which the invoice was entered in the accounting software – however, since the payment was recorded and the check was cut in the month before the period to which the payment relates, it is actually prepaid rent.

The proper way to account for prepaid rent is to record the initial payment in the prepaid assets (or prepaid rent) account, using this entry:

	Debit	Credit
Prepaid assets	$x,xxx	
Accounts payable		$x,xxx

Then, when the check is cut, the accounting software records this entry:

	Debit	Credit
Accounts payable	$x,xxx	
Cash		$x,xxx

Finally, the tenant records the following entry sometime during the month to which the rent payment actually applies, which finally charges the payment to expense:

	Debit	Credit
Rent expense	$x,xxx	
Prepaid assets		$x,xxx

In short, the tenant stores a prepaid rent payment on the balance sheet as an asset until the month when the entity is actually using the facility to which the rent relates, and then charges it to expense.

A concern when recording prepaid rent in this manner is that one might forget to shift the asset into an expense account in the month when rent is consumed. If so, the financial statements under-report the expense and over-report the asset. To avoid this, review the contents of the prepaid assets account prior to closing the books at the end of each month.

Straight-Line Rent

Straight-line rent is the concept that the total lease liability should be charged to expense on an even periodic basis over the term of a lease. The concept is similar to straight-line depreciation, where the cost of an asset is charged to expense on an even basis over the useful life of the asset. The straight-line concept is based on the idea that the usage of a lease is on a consistent basis over time; that is, the leased asset is used at about the same rate from month to month.

To calculate straight-line rent, aggregate the total cost of all lease payments, and divide by the total lease term. The result is the amount to be charged to expense in each month of the lease. This calculation should include all discounts from the normal rent, as well as extra charges that can reasonably be expected to be incurred over the life of the lease.

The calculation of straight-line rent may result in a monthly rent expense for the lessee that differs from the actual amount billed by the lessor. This is usually because the lessor has built escalating lease payments into the lease agreement. In such a case, the straight-line amount charged to expense is higher than the actual amount billed during the first few months of the lease, and lower than the amount billed during the final months of the lease.

This initial disparity, where the amount of the expense is greater than the amount paid, is charged to a deferred liability account. The latter disparity, where the amount paid is greater than the amount of the expense, is a reversal of the accrued liability account. By the end of the lease, the accrued liability account will have a zero balance.

For example, a company enters into a short-term facility lease where the amount billed is $500 per month for the first six months, and $600 per month for the last six months. On a straight-line basis, the amount of rent is $550 per month. In the first month of the lease, the lessee would record a lease expense of $550 (debit), a cash reduction of $500 (credit), and an accrued liability of $50 (credit).

Operating Expense Issues

For certain types of leases (see the Types of Leases section), the tenant is required to pay its share of the operating expenses of a property. This share is typically billed to tenants by the property manager on a monthly basis, using an estimate of what the operating costs will be for the year. At the end of the year, the property manager tallies actual expenses and compares them to the amounts billed to tenants, and either refunds them for overbillings or issues an extra billing if the actual expenses were higher than expected.

The types of costs that the property manager typically bills to tenants, as well as those not usually billed are listed in the following table.

Recoverable and Non-Recoverable Operating Expenses

Recoverable Operating Expenses	Non-Recoverable Operating Expenses
Cleaning fees	Capital improvements
Electricity billings	Depreciation charges
Facility repairs and maintenance	Donations by property management company
Facility staff compensation	Income taxes
Heating, ventilation, and air conditioning maintenance	Interest on debt
Insurance	Leasing costs
Management fees	Legal fees, judgments, and settlements
Property taxes	Marketing costs
Security services	Penalties and fines
Water and sewage fees	

Descriptions of the recoverable operating expenses noted in the last table are as follows:

- *Cleaning fees.* Includes the labor cost of cleaning the common spaces, offices, and grounds of a facility.
- *Electricity billings.* Includes the cost of electricity billed by the local utility. Depending on the metering situation, this charge may be billed to tenants based on their individual usage.
- *Facility repairs and maintenance.* Includes the costs incurred to maintain a property at its intended level of usage, such as the replacement of windows, trim, and light bulbs, or painting over scrapes or repairing the parking lot. This can be a large part of the total operating expenses.
- *Facility staff compensation.* Includes the salaries and wages, payroll taxes, and benefits paid to all staff employed to operate the facility. Examples of these personnel are maintenance staff, bookkeepers, service staff, and property managers.

- *Heating, ventilation and air conditioning (HVAC) maintenance.* Includes the ongoing servicing cost of HVAC, which may reflect either a consistent monthly billing from a provider for preventive maintenance, or separate billings for on-call services.
- *Insurance.* Includes the cost of property insurance, which can cover damage from fires, floods, boiler explosions, and so forth.
- *Management fees.* Includes the cost of the services of a professional real estate management firm, which administers a facility.
- *Property taxes.* A tax charged by the municipality on whose land a property is located. This tax can be the major source of revenue for a municipality, and so can be a large amount.
- *Security services.* Includes the cost of having security staff on-site for surveillance and other activities, as well as of using remote monitoring systems.
- *Water and sewage fees.* Includes the cost of water use and sewage services by the local utility.

Which costs are considered to be recoverable or non-recoverable can be negotiated by tenants, with larger tenants able to shift more costs into the non-recoverable classification.

EXAMPLE

Smith Brothers leases 18,000 square feet of space in the Triangle Building. The property management company estimates that the total recoverable operating expenses of the building in the upcoming calendar year will be $1,000,000. Based on the square footage occupied by Smith Brothers, its share of these operating expenses will be 6% of the total, or $60,000, which calls for a monthly billing of $5,000.

At the end of the year, the property management staff finds that the actual operating costs incurred were $1,050,000. The Smith Brothers share of the $50,000 excess amount is $3,000 (calculated as $50,000 × 6%).

If the lease agreement allows the property management company to classify capital improvements as recoverable operating expenses, the recovery period may be spread over the period during which the improvements are expected to be beneficial to tenants. For example, if an elevator replacement cost $250,000 and was expected to be beneficial to tenants for a ten-year period, then $25,000 of this cost would be included in the recoverable operating expenses classification in each of the next 10 years.

Sub-Leases

A sublease arises when leased property is leased by the original lessee to a third party. When this happens, the original lessee accounts for the sublease as though it were the original lessor. The original lessee continues to account for its ongoing lease payments to the original lessor as though the sublease did not exist.

In rare cases, the new lessee may replace the original lessee. If so, the original lessor accounts for the original lease as a terminated transaction, followed by a new lease with the new lessee that spans the remainder of the lease term.

Presentation and Disclosure Topics

Lease incentives are operating activities, and should be presented within this classification in the statement of cash flows.

If an entity has entered into a lease arrangement, it should disclose the following information in its financial statements:

- *Description.* How contingent rental payments are determined, any renewal, purchase, or escalation clauses, and any restrictions imposed by leasing arrangements.
- *Related parties.* The nature of any leasing transactions with related parties.
- *Rent expense.* The rent expense for every period presented, which should be broken down by minimum, contingent, and sublease rentals.
- *Future payments.* For those leases having minimum lease terms of at least one year, disclose the minimum rental payments for each of the next five years, as well as in aggregate, plus the total amount of minimum sublease rentals to be received in the future.

If the lessor has entered into lease arrangements, disclose the following information in the financial statements:

- *Description.* The company's leasing arrangements, if leasing is a significant part of its business. This includes the carrying amount of property designated for leasing by function and the related amount of accumulated depreciation. Also disclose the minimum future rentals related to noncancelable leases for each of the next five years and in aggregate.
- *Contingent rental income.* The policy for how the lessor records contingent rental income. Note any impact on rental income if the lessor were to defer such income until a triggering event occurs. Also disclose the total amount of contingent rentals included in income for each period presented.
- *Related parties.* The nature of any leasing transactions with related parties.

Summary

The accounting for lease arrangements between lessors and their tenants tends to change little from period to period, and so is not especially difficult for most transactions. The more interesting issues are associated with one-time events, such as how to account for the incentives associated with a new lease, or how to calculate straight-line rent for a new lease. In these cases, consider discussing the proposed accounting entries with the company's auditors, to ensure that the entries will comply with the accounting standards. Once these issues are settled, there should be little additional trouble with ongoing month-to-month payments and receipts.

Chapter 9
Asset Retirement and
Environmental Obligations

Introduction

An asset retirement obligation (ARO) is a liability associated with the retirement of an asset, such as a legal requirement to return a site to its previous condition. The concept of an ARO can be a major issue when owning real estate, since it can involve significant liabilities. The accounting for an ARO, as outlined in this chapter, is concerned with the early recognition of this expense, the subsequent adjustment of this liability as new facts come to light, and eventually settling the obligation.

An example near the end of the chapter illustrates many of the ARO concepts. In addition, this chapter addresses when to record a liability associated with an environmental obligation, how to determine the amount of the liability and the types of costs that should be included in it.

Relevant Accounting Sources

The information stated in this chapter is derived from the following topic in the Accounting Standards Codification:

- Topic 410, *Asset Retirement and Environmental Obligations*

Overview of Asset Retirement Obligations

An organization usually incurs an ARO due to a legal obligation. It may also incur an ARO if a company promises a third party (even the public at large) that it will engage in ARO activities; the circumstances of this promise will drive the determination of whether there is an actual liability. This liability may exist even if there has been no formal action against the company. When making the determination of liability, base the evaluation on current laws, not on projections of what laws there may be in the future, when the asset retirement occurs.

EXAMPLE

Glow Atomic operates an atomic power generation facility, and is required by law to bring the property back to its original condition when the plant is eventually decertified. The company has come under some pressure by various environmental organizations to take the remediation one step further and create a public park on the premises. Because of the significant negative publicity generated by these groups, the company issues a press release in which it commits to create the park. There is no legal requirement for the company to incur this additional expense, so the company's legal counsel should evaluate the facts to determine if there is a legal obligation.

A business should recognize the fair value of an ARO when it incurs the liability, and if it can make a reasonable estimate of the fair value of the ARO.

EXAMPLE

Glow Atomic has completed the construction of an atomic power generation facility, but has not yet taken delivery of fuel rods or undergone certification tests. It will incur an ARO for decontamination, but since it has not yet begun operations, it has not begun to contaminate, and therefore should not yet record an ARO liability.

If a fair value is not initially obtainable, recognize the ARO at a later date, when the fair value becomes available. If a company acquires a property to which an ARO is attached, recognize a liability for the ARO as of the property acquisition date.

If there is not sufficient information available to reasonably estimate the fair value of an ARO, it may be possible to use an expected present value technique that assigns probabilities to cash flows, thereby creating an estimate of the fair value of the ARO. Use an expected present value technique under either of the following scenarios:

- Other parties have specified the settlement date and method of settlement, so that the only uncertainty is whether the obligation will be enforced.
- There is information available from which to estimate the range of possible settlement dates and possible methods of settlement, as well as the probabilities associated with them.

Examples of the sources from which one can obtain the information needed for the preceding estimation requirements are past practice within the company, industry practice, the stated intentions of management, or the estimated useful life of the asset (which indicates a likely ARO settlement date at the end of the useful life).

> **Tip:** The ARO settlement date may be quite a bit further in the future than the useful life of an asset may initially indicate, if the company intends to prolong the useful life with asset upgrades, or has a history of doing so.

If there is an unambiguous requirement that causes an ARO, but there is a low likeli-hood of a performance requirement, it may still be necessary to recognize a liability. When incorporating the low probability of performance into the expected present value calculation for the ARO liability, this will likely reduce the recognized amount of the ARO. Even if there has been a history of non-enforcement of prior AROs for which there was an unambiguous obligation, do not defer the recognition of a liability.

The Initial Measurement of an Asset Retirement Obligation

In most cases, the only way to determine the fair value of an ARO is to use an expected present value technique. When constructing an expected present value of future cash flows, incorporate the following points into the calculation:

- *Discount rate.* Use a credit-adjusted risk-free rate to discount cash flows to their present value. Thus, the credit standing of a business may impact the discount rate used.
- *Probability distribution.* When calculating the expected present value of an ARO, and there are only two possible outcomes, assign a 50 percent proba-bility to each one until there is additional information that alters the initial probability distribution. Otherwise, spread the probability across the full set of possible scenarios.

EXAMPLE

Glow Atomic is compiling the cost of a decontamination ARO several years in the future. It is uncertain of the cost, since supplier fees fluctuate considerably. It arrives at an expected weighted average cash flow based on the following probability analysis:

Cash Flow Estimates	Probability Assessment	Expected Cash Flows
$12,500,000	10%	$1,250,000
15,000,000	15%	2,250,000
16,000,000	50%	8,000,000
22,500,000	25%	5,625,000
	Weighted average cash flows	$17,125,000

Follow these steps in calculating the expected present value of an ARO:

1. Estimate the timing and amount of the cash flows associated with the retire-ment activities.
2. Determine the credit-adjusted risk-free rate.
3. Recognize any period-to-period increase in the carrying amount of the ARO liability as *accretion expense.* To do so, multiply the beginning liability by the credit-adjusted risk-free rate derived when the liability was first measured.

4. Recognize upward liability revisions as a new liability layer, and discount them at the current credit-adjusted risk-free rate.
5. Recognize downward liability revisions by reducing the appropriate liability layer, and discount the reduction at the rate used for the initial recognition of the related liability layer.

When initially recognizing an ARO liability, also capitalize the related asset retirement cost by adding it to the carrying amount of the related asset.

Subsequent Measurement of an Asset Retirement Obligation

It is possible that an ARO liability will not remain static over the life of the related property. Instead, the liability may change over time. If the liability increases, consider the incremental increase in each period to be an additional layer of liability, in addition to any previous liability layers. The following points will assist in the recognition of these additional layers:

- Initially recognize each layer at its fair value.

EXAMPLE

Glow Atomic has been operating an atomic power plant for three years. It initially recognized an ARO of $250 million for the eventual dismantling of the plant after its useful life has ended. In the fifth year, Glow detects groundwater contamination, and recognizes an additional layer of ARO liability for $20 million to deal with it. In the seventh year, a leak in the sodium cooling lines causes overheating and a significant release of radioactive steam that impacts 50 square miles of land downwind from the facility. Glow recognizes an additional layer of ARO liability of $150 million to address this issue.

- Systematically allocate the ARO liability to expense over the useful life of the underlying asset.
- Measure changes in the liability due to the passage of time, using the credit-adjusted risk-free rate when each layer of liability was first recognized. Recognize this cost as an increase in the liability. When charged to expense, this is classified as accretion expense (which is not the same as interest expense).
- As the time period shortens before an ARO is realized, the assessment of the timing, amount, and probabilities associated with cash flows will improve. It will likely be necessary to alter the ARO liability based on these changes in estimate. If there is an upward revision in the ARO liability, discount it using the current credit-adjusted risk-free rate. If there is a downward revision in the ARO liability, discount it using the original credit-adjusted risk-free rate when the liability layer was first recognized. If it is not possible to identify the liability layer to which the downward adjustment relates, use a weighted-average credit-adjusted risk-free rate to discount it.

Settlement of an Asset Retirement Obligation

An ARO is normally settled only when the underlying asset is retired, though it is possible that some portion of an ARO will be settled prior to asset retirement.

If it becomes apparent that no expenses will be required as part of the retirement of an asset, reverse any remaining unamortized ARO to zero.

> **Tip:** If a company cannot fulfill its ARO responsibilities and a third party does so instead, this does not relieve the company from recording an ARO liability, on the grounds that it may now have an obligation to pay the third party instead.

EXAMPLE

Glow Atomic operates an atomic power generation facility, and is legally required to decontaminate the facility when it is decommissioned in five years. Glow uses the following assumptions about the ARO:

- The decontamination cost is $90 million.
- The risk-free rate is 5%, to which Glow adds 3% to reflect the effect of its credit standing.
- The assumed rate of inflation over the five-year period is four percent.

With an average inflation rate of 4% per year for the next five years, the current decontamination cost of $90 million increases to approximately $109.5 million by the end of the fifth year. The expected present value of the $109.5 million payout, using the 8% credit-adjusted risk-free rate, is $74,524,000 (calculated as $109.5 million × 0.68058 discount rate).

Glow then calculates the amount of annual accretion using the 8% rate, as shown in the following table:

Year	Beginning Liability	Accretion	Ending Liability
1	$74,524,000	$5,962,000	$80,486,000
2	80,486,000	6,439,000	86,925,000
3	86,925,000	6,954,000	93,879,000
4	93,879,000	7,510,000	101,389,000
5	101,389,000	8,111,000	109,500,000

Glow then combines the accretion expense with the straight-line depreciation expense noted in the following table to show how all components of the ARO are charged to expense over the next five years. Note that the accretion expense is carried forward from the preceding table. The depreciation is based on the $74,524,000 present value of the ARO, spread evenly over five years.

Year	Accretion Expense	Depreciation Expense	Total Expense
1	$5,962,000	$14,904,800	$20,866,800
2	6,439,000	14,904,800	21,343,800
3	6,954,000	14,904,800	21,858,800
4	7,510,000	14,904,800	22,414,800
5	8,111,000	14,904,800	23,015,800
			$109,500,000

After the plant is closed, Glow commences its decontamination activities. The actual cost is $115 million.

Here is a selection of the journal entries that Glow recorded over the term of the ARO:

	Debit	Credit
Facility decontamination asset	90,000,000	
Asset retirement obligation liability		90,000,000
To record the initial fair value of the asset retirement obligation		

	Debit	Credit
Depreciation expense	14,904,800	
Accumulated depreciation		14,904,800
To record the annual depreciation on the asset retirement obligation		

	Debit	Credit
Accretion expense	As noted in schedule	
Asset retirement obligation liability		As noted in schedule
To record the annual accretion expense on the asset retirement obligation liability		

	Debit	Credit
Loss on ARO settlement	5,500,000	
Remediation expense		5,500,000
To record settlement of the excess asset retirement obligation		

Overview of Environmental Obligations

There are a number of federal laws that impose an obligation on a business to remediate sites that contain environmentally hazardous conditions, as well as to control or prevent pollution. Remediation can include feasibility studies, cleanup costs, legal fees, government oversight costs, and restoration costs.

In total, these laws can create a serious liability for a business, to the extent of causing the business to go bankrupt. Consider, for example, the extent of liability associated with a Superfund site, where liability can be associated with:

- The current owner or operator of the site
- Previous owners or operators of the site at the time of disposal of hazardous substances
- Parties that arranged for the disposal of hazardous substances found at the site
- Parties that transported hazardous substances to the site

The level of liability imposed by other environmental laws may not be as all-encompassing as the Superfund liability, but the level of liability imposed can still be crushing. Accordingly, the accounting for environmental obligations must be well documented, in order to convey the full scope of the liability.

In general, a liability for an environmental obligation should be accrued if both of the following circumstances are present:

- It is probable that an asset has been impaired or a liability has been incurred. This is based on both of the following criteria:
  - An assertion has been made that the business bears responsibility for a past event; and
  - It is probable that the outcome of the assertion will be unfavorable to the business.
- The amount of the loss or a loss range can be reasonably estimated.

It is recognized that the liability associated with environmental obligations can change dramatically over time, depending on the number and type of hazardous substances involved, the financial condition of other responsible parties, and other factors. Accordingly, the recorded liability associated with environmental obligations can change. Further, it may not be possible to initially estimate some components of the liability, which does not prevent other components of the liability from being recognized as soon as possible.

EXAMPLE

Glow Atomic has been notified by the government that it must conduct a remedial investigation and feasibility study for a Superfund site to which it sent uranium waste products in the past. There is sufficient information to estimate the cost of the study, for which Glow records an accrued liability. However, there is no way to initially determine the extent of any additional liabilities associated with the site until the study has at least commenced. Accordingly, Glow continually reviews the preliminary findings of the study, and updates the liability for its environmental obligation based on changes in that information.

Once there is information available regarding the extent of an environmental obligation, a business should record its best estimate of the liability. If it is not possible to create a best estimate, then at least a minimum estimate of the liability should be recorded. The estimate is refined as better information becomes available.

In some cases, it is possible to derive a reasonable estimate of liability quite early in the remediation process, because it is similar to the remediation that a business has encountered at other sites. In these instances, the full amount of the liability should be recognized at once.

The costs associated with the treatment of environmental contamination costs should be charged to expense in nearly all cases. The sole exceptions are:

- The costs incurred will increase the capacity of the property, or extend its life, or improve its safety or efficiency
- The costs incurred are needed to prepare a property for sale that is currently classified as held for sale
- The costs improve the property, as well as mitigate or prevent environmental contamination that has yet to occur and that might otherwise arise from future operations

---

EXAMPLE

Armadillo Industries spends $250,000 to construct a concrete pad that is designed to prevent fluid leaks from causing groundwater contamination. Making this investment improves the safety of the property, while also preventing future environmental contamination. Consequently, Armadillo can capitalize the $250,000 cost of the concrete pad, and should depreciate it over the remaining useful life of the property.

Measurement of Environmental Obligations

In order to determine the extent of the liability associated with an environmental obligation, follow these steps:

1. Identify those parties likely to be considered responsible for the site requiring remediation. These potentially responsible parties may include the following:

   - Participating parties
   - Recalcitrant parties
   - Unproven parties
   - Unknown parties
   - Orphan share parties

2. Determine the likelihood that those parties will pay their share of the liability associated with site remediation, based primarily on their financial condition. There is a presumption that costs will only be allocated among the participating responsible parties, since the other parties are less likely to pay their shares of the liability.

3. Based on the preceding steps, calculate the percentage of the total liability that the company should record. The sources for this information can include the liability percentages that the responsible parties have agreed to, or which have been assigned by a consultant, or which have been assigned by the Environmental Protection Agency (EPA). If the company chooses to record the liability in a different amount, it should be based on objective, verifiable information, examples of which are:

    *   Existing data about the types and amounts of waste at the site
    *   Prior experience with liability allocations in comparable situations
    *   Reports issued by environmental specialists
    *   Internal data that refutes EPA allegations

EXAMPLE

Armadillo Industries has been notified by the EPA that it is a potentially responsible party in a groundwater contamination case. The EPA has identified three companies as being potentially responsible. The three parties employ an arbitrator to allocate the responsibility for costs among the companies. The arbitrator derives the following allocations:

	Allocation Percentage
Armadillo Industries	40%
Boxcar Munitions	20%
Chelsea Chemicals	20%
	80%
Recalcitrant share (nonparticipating parties)	15%
Orphan share (no party can be identified)	5%
Total	100%

The total estimated remediation cost is estimated to be $5 million. Armadillo's direct share of this amount is $2 million (calculated as $5 million total remediation × 40% share). Also, Armadillo should record a liability for its share of those amounts allocated to other parties who are not expected to pay their shares, which is $500,000 (calculated as half of the total allocation for responsible parties × the cost allocated to the recalcitrant and orphan shares).

The costs that should be included in a company's liability for environmental obligations include the following:

*   Direct remediation activity costs, such as investigations, risk assessments, remedial actions, activities related to government oversight, and post-remediation monitoring.
*   The compensation and related benefit costs for those employees expected to spend a significant amount of their time on remediation activities.

When measuring these costs, do so for the estimated time periods during which activities will occur, which means that an inflation factor should be included for periods further in the future. It may also be possible to include a productivity factor that is caused by gaining experience with remediation efforts over time, and which may reduce mitigation costs. When it is not possible to estimate the costs of inflation, perhaps due to uncertainties about the timing of expenditures, it is acceptable to initially record costs at their current-cost estimates, and adjust them later, as more precise information becomes available.

Any costs related to routine environmental compliance activities, as well as any litigation costs associated with potential recoveries, are not considered part of the remediation effort, and so are not included in the environmental obligation liability. These costs are to be charged to expense as incurred.

Changes in the environmental liability are especially likely when there are multiple parties involved, since additional parties may be added over time, or the apportionment of liability between parties may change. Also, estimates of the exact amount of cost incurred will change continually. For these reasons, the amount of liability recorded for environmental obligations will almost certainly not be the exact amount that is eventually incurred, and so will have to be updated at regular intervals. If so, each update is treated as a change in estimate, which means that there is no retroactive change in the liability reported by a business; instead, the change is recorded only on a go-forward basis.

Recoveries Related to Environmental Obligations

It is possible that a business may contact other entities concerning the recovery of funds expended on environmental remediation, on the grounds that the other entities are liable for the remediation (or are liable because they are insurers).

The recognition of an asset related to the recovery of an environmental obligation should not be made unless recovery of the claimed amount is considered probable and the amount can be reasonably estimated. If a claim is currently the subject of litigation, it is reasonable to assume that recovery of the claim is not probable, and so should not be recognized.

A recovery can be recorded at its undiscounted amount if the liability is not discounted, and the timing of the recovery is dependent on the timing of the liability payment. This will be the case in most situations, so the recovery will generally be recorded at its undiscounted amount.

Presentation and Disclosure Topics

This section contains the disclosures for various aspects of asset retirement and environmental obligations that are required under GAAP. At the end of each set of requirements is a sample disclosure containing the more common elements of the requirements.

Asset Retirement Obligations

If a company's assets are subject to asset retirement obligations, disclose the following information:

- *Description.* Describe any asset retirement obligations, as well as the assets with which they are associated.
- *Fair values.* Disclose the fair values of any assets that are legally restricted for purposes of setting asset retirement obligations. If it is not possible to reasonably estimate the fair value of an asset retirement obligation, state the reasons for this estimation difficulty.
- *Reconciliation.* Present a reconciliation of the beginning and ending carrying amounts of all asset retirement obligations, in aggregate, showing the changes attributable to the following items:
  - Accretion expense
  - Liabilities incurred in the reporting period
  - Liabilities settled in the reporting period
  - Revisions to estimated cash flows

EXAMPLE

Suture Corporation discloses the following information about its asset retirement obligations:

The company records the fair value of a liability for an asset retirement obligation (ARO) that is recorded when there is a legal obligation associated with the retirement of a tangible long-lived asset and the liability can be reasonably estimated. The recording of ARO primarily affects the company's accounting for its mining of properties in Nevada for various substances used in its medical research. The company performs periodic reviews of its assets for any changes in the facts and circumstances that might require recognition of a retirement obligation.

The following table indicates the changes to the company's before-tax asset retirement obligations in 20X3, 20X2, and 20X1:

(000s)	20X3	20X2	20X1
Balance at January 1	$5,350	$4,450	$2,900
Liabilities assumed in ABC acquisition	--	--	1,200
Liabilities incurred	200	250	100
Liabilities settled	(1,000)	(400)	(200)
Accretion expense	270	250	300
Revisions in estimated cash flows	1,320	800	150
Balance at December 31	$6,140	$5,350	$4,450

In the preceding table, the amounts for 20X2 and 20X3 associated with "Revisions in estimated cash flows" reflect increased cost estimates to abandon the Harkness Mine in Nevada, due to increased regulatory requirements.

Environmental Obligations

The expenses associated with environmental obligations are recorded as part of operating expenses, on the grounds that environmental remediation is considered a regular cost of doing business. Credits from the recovery of environmental costs are also to be recorded within operating expenses.

If a business has recorded environmental obligations, disclose the following information:

- *Discounting*. Note whether the liability is measured on a discounted basis, the undiscounted amount, and the discount rate used. This is the only disclosure required for environmental obligations.
- *Obligation description*. Companies are encouraged to disclose the circumstances triggering a liability, as well as any policy related to the timing of recognition of recoveries.
- *Loss contingencies*. Disclosure of environmental remediation loss contingencies is encouraged.
- *Liability detail*. Companies are encouraged to disclose additional information about their environmental liabilities, including:
  - The time frame of disbursements
  - The time frame for realization of recognized probable recoveries
  - The reasons why losses cannot be estimated
  - If information about a specific remediation obligation is relevant to understanding the financial statements, note the amount accrued for that site, the nature of any reasonably possible loss contingency and an estimate of the possible loss, whether other potentially responsible parties are involved and the company's share of the obligation, the status of regulatory proceedings, and the time period during which the contingency is likely to be resolved.
  - The expense related to environmental remediation loss contingencies, the amount of any expense reduction caused by recoveries from third parties, and the income statement caption in which these costs and reductions are included.
- *Impact of laws and regulations*. Companies are encouraged to provide a description of the applicability and financial impact of environmental laws and regulations on their business, as well as how this may cause loss contingencies related to the remediation of environmental issues in the future.

EXAMPLE

Armadillo Industries has been notified of its liability to decontaminate the soil at one of its facilities, for which it provides the following disclosure in its financial statements:

> Armadillo has begun a decontamination project related to the soil near its Central City facility. The company estimates that the cost of the project will be at least $1.8 million, and has accrued the entire amount of this expense as an operating expense. The total cost of the project will depend on the amount of soil contamination found as the project progresses, and may be as much as $3.2 million. The company expects that all remediation activities will have been completed within two years.

Summary

The accounting for an asset retirement obligation can be complex, especially if there are multiple liability layers and changes to those layers occur with some frequency. Because of the additional accounting effort required to track AROs, it makes sense to use every effort to avoid the recognition of an ARO within the boundaries set by GAAP. In many cases, the amount of an ARO will likely be so minimal as to not require recognition. However, in such industries as mining, chemicals, and power generation, the concept of the ARO is of great concern, and forms a significant proportion of a company's total liabilities.

Environmental obligations can strike any organization, large or small, and can result in a massive liability. The accounting for this liability is not especially difficult. However, given its considerable impact on a company's financial results, it is necessary to thoroughly document the calculation of all recorded environmental liabilities, as well as the justification for *not* recording any additional liabilities.

Chapter 10
Real Estate Ventures

Introduction

A large investment may be required to fund a real estate project, so it is common for more than one entity to contribute funds to it. This is particularly common when an investment is perceived to be risky, so that the possibility of loss can be spread among several investors. These ventures can be organized in a variety of ways, such as:

- Several actively participating partners
- A syndication of passive investors who contribute funds and let a general partner manage all activities

There are a number of accounting issues related to real estate ventures, including how the investors account for their investments in a venture, ongoing transactions between investors and a venture, the compensation paid to syndicators, and participating mortgage loans. These topics and more are addressed in the following sections.

Relevant Accounting Sources

The information stated in this chapter is derived from the following topics in the Accounting Standards Codification:

- Topic 323, *Investments – Equity Method and Joint Ventures*
- Topic 805, *Business Combinations*
- Topic 850, *Related Party Disclosures*
- Topic 970, *Real Estate - General*

Accounting for an Interest in a Real Estate Venture

When an investor has made an investment in a real estate venture, there are three possible ways in which to account for this ownership interest. The alternatives are:

- *Consolidation.* Used when the investor has a majority voting interest in another entity. It requires that the financial statements of the parent entity and its subsidiaries be combined.
- *Equity method of accounting.* Used when the investor has a 20% - 50% ownership interest in a venture, or a lesser ownership percentage but significant influence over the venture.
- *Cost method.* Used when the investment in a venture is less than 20% or the investor has no influence over the management of the venture.

Further explanations of these methods are described in the following sections.

Control is considered to exist when the investor owns a majority voting interest in an entity. If the partnership voting interests in a general partnership are not clearly indicated, then an alternative indicator of control is when the investor owns over 50 percent of the profits or losses generated by the partnership. Control can also exist by court order, or by agreement with the other partners in the partnership. Conversely, control may not exist when other partners have substantive rights that allow them to participate in significant operating decisions of the partnership.

No consolidation is required when the investor is a limited partner in a partnership. However, if the reporting entity is a general partner in a partnership, it is presumed to have control, and so should consolidate. If there are multiple general partners, determine which one has control by examining the relevant facts and circumstances of the arrangement.

In rare cases, additional rights given to limited partners overcome the assumption that a general partner has control of a partnership. This is the case when a simple majority (or less) vote of the limited partners can trigger one or more of the following events, without there being any significant barriers to doing so:

- Dissolve the partnership
- Remove the general partners without cause

EXAMPLE

There are 10 limited partners in the Altman Partnership, each holding an equal interest. Under the terms of the partnership agreement, a simple majority of the partners is required to remove the general partner, which therefore requires six favorable votes. If the partnership agreement had instead required at least seven votes in favor, this would be a supermajority requirement, and there would be no presumption that the limited partners control the partnership.

Barriers to such a vote that are considered significant include only being able to vote within a narrow time window, incurring a financial penalty, and the absence of a mechanism for the limited partners to conduct a vote.

The general partners may also not have control over a partnership when the limited partners have substantive participating rights. These rights allow limited partners to participate in certain decisions regarding the finances and operations of a partnership in the ordinary course of business. Examples of such decisions are setting management compensation, selecting or terminating managers, and establishing budgets. Examples of decisions that are *not* considered substantive are the right to select the name of the partnership, the location of its headquarters, and the selection of its outside auditors. The limited partners are not considered to have substantive participating rights when the general partners have the right to buy them out at fair value or less, and this option is prudent, feasible, and within the control of the general partners.

If the rights noted in this section are substantive, then the general partners are considered to not have control. In this situation, the general partners would not consolidate; instead, they should each use the equity method to account for their participation in the partnership.

Consolidations

Consolidation accounting is the process of combining the financial results of several subsidiary companies into the combined financial results of the parent company. Consolidated financial statements require considerable effort to construct, since they must exclude the impact of any transactions between the entities being reported on. Thus, if there is a sale of goods between the subsidiaries of a parent company, this intercompany sale must be eliminated from the consolidated financial statements. Another common intercompany elimination is when the parent company pays interest income to the subsidiaries whose cash it is using to make investments; this interest income must be eliminated from the consolidated financial statements.

The following steps document the consolidation accounting process flow, with a few steps eliminated that are unlikely to be needed for a consolidation with a real estate venture:

1. *Record intercompany loans.* If the parent company has been consolidating the cash balances of its subsidiaries into an investment account, record intercompany loans from the subsidiaries to the parent company. Also record an interest income allocation for the interest earned on consolidated investments from the parent company down to the subsidiaries.
2. *Charge corporate overhead.* If the parent company allocates its overhead costs to subsidiaries, calculate the amount of the allocation and charge it to the various subsidiaries.
3. *Charge payables.* If the parent company runs a consolidated payables operation, verify that all accounts payable recorded during the period have been appropriately charged to the various subsidiaries.
4. *Charge payroll expenses.* If the parent company has been using a common paymaster system to pay all employees throughout the company, ensure that the proper allocation of payroll expenses has been made to all subsidiaries.
5. *Complete adjusting entries.* At the subsidiary and corporate levels, record any adjusting entries needed to properly record revenue and expense transactions in the correct period.
6. *Investigate asset, liability, and equity account balances.* Verify that the contents of all asset, liability, and equity accounts for both the subsidiaries and the corporate parent are correct, and adjust as necessary.
7. *Review subsidiary financial statements.* Print and review the financial statements for each subsidiary, and investigate any items that appear to be unusual or incorrect. Make adjustments as necessary.

8. *Eliminate intercompany transactions.* If there have been any intercompany transactions, reverse them at the parent company level to eliminate their effects from the consolidated financial statements. Examples of intercompany transactions are:

- Security holdings
- Debt
- Sales (with the reversal of related inventory amounts)
- Purchases (with the reversal of related inventory amounts)
- Interest
- Dividends
- Gains or losses on asset sales

9. *Eliminate subsidiary retained earnings.* Remove the retained earnings of each subsidiary as of its acquisition date from the consolidated financial statements.

10. *Eliminate parent shares held by subsidiary.* If a subsidiary holds shares in the parent entity, these are not treated as outstanding shares in the consolidated balance sheet. Instead, they are considered to be treasury stock.

11. *Defer taxes on inter-company profits.* If income taxes have already been paid on inter-company profits, defer them in the consolidated financial statements. An alternative treatment is to reduce the amount of the inter-entity profits to be eliminated by the amount of the taxes.

12. *Review parent financial statements.* Print and review the financial statements for the parent company, and investigate any items that appear to be unusual or incorrect. Make adjustments as necessary.

13. *Close subsidiary books.* Depending upon the accounting software in use, it may be necessary to access the financial records of each subsidiary and flag them as closed. This prevents any additional transactions from being recorded in the accounting period being closed.

14. *Close parent company books.* Flag the parent company accounting period as closed, so that no additional transactions can be reported in the accounting period being closed.

15. *Issue financial statements.* Print and distribute the consolidated financial statements.

If a subsidiary uses a different currency as its operating currency, an additional consolidation accounting step is to convert its financial statements into the operating currency of the parent company.

Given the number of steps, it is useful to convert them into a detailed procedure, which the accounting department should follow religiously as part of its closing process. Otherwise, a key step could be missed, which would throw off the financial statement results.

Consolidation Examples

This section contains a number of examples that clarify the consolidation outcome for different situations. Each situation is dealt with in a different sub-section.

Recognition of Noncontrolling Interest

A parent company may find it necessary to sell a share of its ownership interest in a subsidiary to a third party. This event can trigger the recognition of a gain or loss if the amount of the sale differs from the carrying amount of the equity. It will also result in the recognition of a noncontrolling interest, as noted in the following example.

EXAMPLE

Blitz Partners owns all 100,000 the outstanding shares of Pronto Real Estate. The carrying amount of the equity of Pronto is $1,000,000.

Blitz needs new financing for other investments, and so elects to sell 30,000 of its Pronto shares to a third party for $350,000 in cash. This transaction reduces the ownership of Blitz in Pronto to a 70% interest. This change in ownership is accounted for by recognizing a noncontrolling interest of $300,000, which is calculated as follows:

$1,000,000 Carrying amount of equity × 30% Interest = $300,000

The remaining $50,000 that Blitz received from the third party is recognized as an increase in additional paid-in capital for Blitz.

Sale of Shares by Subsidiary

The managers of a subsidiary may find it necessary to sell shares to third parties. Doing so will reduce the ownership interest of the parent entity. When this happens, multiply the newly-adjusted ownership interest of the parent by the carrying amount of the subsidiary's new equity balance to arrive at the revised investment of the parent in the subsidiary. This situation is addressed in the following example.

EXAMPLE

Higher Properties has 50,000 shares of common stock outstanding. Of this amount, 40,000 shares are owned by its parent, Milton Brothers, and the remaining shares are owned by unrelated third parties. The carrying amount of the equity of Higher is $1,000,000. Of the $1,000,000, 80% (or $800,000) is attributed to Milton, and 20% (or $200,000) to the noncontrolling interest in Higher.

Higher is in need of additional funding, and elects to sell 10,000 shares to an unrelated third party for $220,000. This transaction reduces Milton's ownership interest in Higher to 67%, which is calculated as:

40,000 Shares owned by Milton ÷ 60,000 Total shares outstanding = 66.67%

As a result of the stock sale, Higher's equity has increased from $1,000,000 to $1,220,000. Milton's share of this increased equity is 66.67%, which is $813,374. This means that Milton recognizes an increase of $13,374 in its Higher investment, with a corresponding increase in its additional paid-in capital. The noncontrolling interest in Higher is now $406,626, which is calculated as follows:

$1,220,000 Carrying amount of equity × 33.33% Ownership interest = $406,626

The combined ownership amounts of Milton and the noncontrolling interests equal $1,220,000, which matches the total carrying amount of Higher's equity.

Share of Accumulated Other Comprehensive Income

A subsidiary may carry on its books an accumulated other comprehensive income balance. This account is used to accumulate unrealized gains and unrealized losses on those line items in the income statement that are classified within the other comprehensive income category. A transaction is unrealized when it has not yet been settled. Thus, if a subsidiary were to invest in a bond, it would record any gain or loss in its fair value in other comprehensive income until it sells the bond, at which time the gain or loss would be realized, and then shifted out of the accumulated other comprehensive income account.

A noncontrolling interest is assigned a proportional share of the balance in the accumulated other comprehensive income account. If the ownership percentages of the controlling and noncontrolling interests change, then the proportional assignment of the balance in this account must also change. The following example illustrates the concept.

EXAMPLE

Lantern Developments is a subsidiary of Camelot Fund. Lantern has 25,000 shares of common stock outstanding, of which 20,000 shares are owned by Camelot and 5,000 by a third party that has a noncontrolling interest in Lantern. The carrying amount of the noncontrolling interest is $40,000, which includes $10,000 of accumulated other comprehensive income.

Camelot pays $20,000 to acquire half of the noncontrolling interest. As a result of this transaction, Camelot has increased its ownership percentage of Lantern to 90% from the prior 80% level. The accounting for the transaction is a reduction of the noncontrolling interest to $20,000 (half of the previous amount). Also, Camelot's share of the accumulated other comprehensive income that had been ascribed to the noncontrolling interest is $5,000 (half of the total). This transfer is accomplished with an offsetting decrease in the additional paid-in capital attributable to Camelot.

Full Consolidation Example

The following example combines a number of issues, including the sale and subsequent partial re-purchase of a noncontrolling interest, and the assignment of accumulated other comprehensive income.

EXAMPLE

Icelandic Investments has a subsidiary, Canadian Clubs. During 20X2, Icelandic owns all of the 50,000 shares outstanding for Canadian, so its ownership interest in Canadian is 100%.

In February of 20X2, Canadian purchases $250,000 of securities and classifies them as available for sale. By the end of the year, the carrying amount of these securities has increased to $260,000. For the full year, Canadian earned net profits of $300,000. As of year-end, the detail of Canadian's equity was as follows:

Common stock	$50,000
Additional paid-in capital	100,000
Retained earnings	350,000
Accumulated other comprehensive income	10,000
Total equity	$510,000

On the first day of the new year, Icelandic elects to sell 10% of its interest in Canadian, so it sells 5,000 shares to a third party for $60,000. In the consolidated financial statements of the entities, the sale of stock is accounted for as follows:

- Recognize a noncontrolling interest of $51,000 (calculated as $510,000 total equity × 10%).
- Recognize an increase in the additional paid-in capital of Icelandic of $9,000, which is the difference between the $60,000 cash received from the third party and the $51,000 carrying amount of the noncontrolling interest.

- Recognize an increase in the additional paid-in capital of Icelandic of $1,000, and a matching reduction of its accumulated other comprehensive income. This change reflects the carrying amount of Canadian's $10,000 of accumulated other comprehensive income related to the available for sale securities, of which 10% is now assigned to the noncontrolling interest.
- These activities result in the following journal entry:

	Debit	Credit
Cash	60,000	
Accumulated other comprehensive income (Icelandic)	1,000	
Noncontrolling interest		51,000
Additional paid-in capital (Icelandic)		10,000

For the year ended 20X3, Canadian does not enjoy as large a profit; its net profit is $100,000. At year-end, the carrying amount of the noncontrolling interest is $64,000, of which $3,000 is accumulated other comprehensive income.

Immediately following year-end, Icelandic thinks better of its earlier decision to sell Canadian shares to a third party, and negotiates to repurchase half of the shares (2,500 shares) for $40,000. This results in an increase in Icelandic's ownership of Canadian to 95%.

Icelandic accounts for this purchase of stock for the consolidated financial statements through the following steps:

- Recognize a reduction of the noncontrolling interest of $25,500 (calculated as $51,000 noncontrolling interest × 50%).
- Recognize a reduction in the additional paid-in capital of Icelandic of $14,500, which is the difference between the $40,000 paid to the third party and the $25,500 reduction in the carrying amount of the noncontrolling interest.
- Recognize a $1,500 reduction in the additional paid-in capital account of Icelandic, which is 50% of the carrying amount of the accumulated other comprehensive income formerly attributed to the third party, which has been repurchased by Icelandic. The offset to this transaction is an increase of $1,500 in the accumulated other comprehensive income attributable to Icelandic.
- These activities result in the following journal entry:

	Debit	Credit
Noncontrolling interest	25,500	
Additional paid-in capital (Icelandic)	16,000	
Accumulated other comprehensive income (Icelandic)		1,500
Cash		40,000

Equity Method of Accounting

The equity method is designed to measure changes in the economic results of a venture by requiring the investor to recognize its share of the profits or losses recorded by the venture.

The essential accounting under the equity method is to initially recognize an investment in a venture at cost, and then adjust the carrying amount of the investment by recognizing its share of the earnings or losses of the venture in earnings over time. The following additional guidance applies to these basic points:

- *Dividends*. The investor subtracts any dividends received from the venture from the carrying amount of the investor's investment in the venture.
- *Financial statement issuance*. The investor can only account for its share of the earnings or losses of the venture if the venture issues financial statements. This may result in occasional lags in reporting.
- *Funding of prior losses*. If the investor pays the venture with the intent of offsetting prior venture losses, and the carrying amount of the investor's interest in the venture has already been reduced to zero, then the investor's share of any additional losses can be applied against the additional funds paid to the venture.
- *Impairment*. The investor should write down its investment in a venture if there is an other-than-temporary decline in value of the investment. This situation can arise when other investors refuse to continue supporting the venture or the venture generates minimal earnings.
- *Intra-entity profits and losses*. Eliminate all intra-entity profits that relate to the investor's ownership of the venture. An investor that controls the venture and then enters into a business transaction with the venture must eliminate all of the inter-entity profit on assets remaining within the group.

EXAMPLE

Bitumen Brothers sells a $2,000,000 property to Aardvark Enterprises, in which Bitumen owns a 40% interest. The profit on the deal is $200,000. Bitumen can only recognize 60% of the profit, which relates to the 60% ownership of Aardvark that is held by other parties. Thus, Bitumen can only recognize a profit of $120,000 on the transaction.

- *Venture losses*. It is possible that the investor's share of the losses of a venture will exceed the carrying amount of its investment in the venture. If so, the investor should report losses up to its carrying amount, as well as any additional financial support given to the venture, and then discontinue use of the equity method. However, additional losses can be recorded if it appears assured that the venture will shortly return to profitability. If there is a return to profitability, the investor can return to the equity method only after its share of the profits has been offset by those losses not recognized when use of the equity method was halted.

EXAMPLE

Ironton Associates is a noncontrolling investor in Corrugated Investment Properties. Corrugated is in the process of developing a series of low-income housing properties in inner city locations. Corrugated has incurred $20,000,000 of start-up losses, but occupancy rates are accelerating, and the business is expected to initially become profitable within the next three months.

Ironton's share of the start-up losses has reduced its investment in Corrugated under the equity method to zero. However, because of the expectation of profits in the near future, Ironton should continue to record its share of Corrugated's losses.

- *Other comprehensive income.* The investor should record its proportionate share of the venture's equity adjustments related to other comprehensive income. The entry is an adjustment to the investment account, with an offsetting adjustment in equity. If the investor discontinues its use of the equity method, offset the existing proportionate share of these equity adjustments against the carrying value of the investment. If the result of this netting is a value in the carrying amount of less than zero, charge the excess amount to income. Also, stop recording the investor's proportionate share of the equity adjustments related to other comprehensive income in future periods.
- *Other write-downs.* If an investor's investment in a venture has been written down to zero, but it has other investments in the venture, the investor should continue to report its share of any additional venture losses, and offset them against the other investments, in sequence of the seniority of those investments (with offsets against the most junior items first). If the venture generates income at a later date, the investor should apply its share of these profits to the other investments in order, with application going against the most senior items first.
- *Other obligations.* If the investor has an obligation to provide additional financial support to the venture, then the investor should continue to recognize its share of venture losses in excess of its investment. Examples of additional financial support are:
  - The investor has issued a guarantee on behalf of the venture.
  - The investor has indicated a commitment to provide more financial support; this might be based on having previously provided support or having made statements to third parties to do so.
- *Share calculation.* The proportion of the venture's earnings or losses to be recognized by the investor is based on the investor's holdings of common stock and in-substance common stock.
- *Share issuances.* If the venture issues shares, the investor should account for the transaction as if a proportionate share of its own investment in the venture had been sold. If there is a gain or loss resulting from the stock sale, recognize it in earnings.

- *Unrealized fair value increases.* If there is an unrealized increase in the estimated fair value of the venture's assets, do not offset any losses against them.

EXAMPLE

Armadillo Holdings acquires a 30% interest in Squirrel Properties. Armadillo is a noncontrolling investor, so it uses the equity method to account for the investment. In the next year, Squirrel earns $400,000. Armadillo records its 30% share of the profit with the following entry:

	Debit	Credit
Investment in Squirrel Properties	120,000	
Equity in Squirrel Properties income		120,000

A few months later, Squirrel issues a $50,000 cash dividend to Armadillo, which the company records with the following entry:

	Debit	Credit
Cash	50,000	
Investment in Titanium Barriers		50,000

EXAMPLE

Armadillo Holdings has a 35% ownership interest in Buck Properties. The carrying amount of this investment has been reduced to zero because of previous losses. To keep Buck solvent, Armadillo has purchased $250,000 of Buck's preferred stock, and extended a long-term unsecured loan of $500,000.

During the next year, Buck incurs a $1,200,000 loss, of which Armadillo's share is 35%, or $420,000. Since the next most senior level of Buck's capital after common stock is its preferred stock, Armadillo first offsets its share of the loss against its preferred stock investment. Doing so reduces the carrying amount of the preferred stock to zero, leaving $170,000 to be applied against the carrying amount of the loan. This results in the following entry by Armadillo:

	Debit	Credit
Equity method loss	420,000	
Preferred stock investment		250,000
Loan		170,000

In the following year, Buck records $800,000 of profits, of which Armadillo's share is $280,000. Armadillo applies the $280,000 first against the loan write-down, and then against the preferred stock write-down with the following entry:

	Debit	Credit
Preferred stock investment	110,000	
Loan	170,000	
Equity method income		280,000

The result is that the carrying amount of the loan is fully restored, while the carrying amount of the preferred stock investment is still reduced by $140,000 from its original level.

A unique situation arises when other investors in a real estate venture cannot bear their share of any losses incurred by the venture. In this case, losses are not considered to be allocable to these financially shaky investors. Instead, each remaining investor should record a proportionate share of the unallocated losses. This accounting does not apply to situations where there is real property, jointly owned and operated as undivided interests, *and* the claims of investor creditors are limited to the respective investor interests in the property. If the venture generates income at a later date, the investor should record its proportionate share of the profits that would normally have been allocated to those investors that could not bear their share of the earlier venture losses. These additional profits should be recognized until they offset the excess losses that had previously been recorded.

Note: An investor should only record an additional loss that would normally be allocated to another investor when it is *probable* that the other investor cannot bear the loss.

EXAMPLE

Smith & Sons is a noncontrolling investor in Bipartisan Real Estate Investments. Bipartisan has generated a loss of $1,000,000, of which Smith's share is $150,000. In addition, Smith evaluates the ability of the other investors in Bipartisan to bear their share of the losses. Smith compiles the following information:

	Previously Made Loans to Support Cash Deficits	Has a Satisfactory Credit Rating	Has Provided Collateralized Guarantees
Grabber Investments	√		√
Ichabod Family Investments	×	×	×
Turncoat Family Fund	√	√	

The information in the table indicates that Ichabod Family Investments may not be able to bear its share of Bipartisan losses, which could require the other investors to record their proportionate shares of the losses normally apportioned to Ichabod.

Cost Method

The cost method mandates that the investor account for an investment in a venture at its historical cost (i.e., the purchase price). This information appears as an asset on the balance sheet of the investor.

Once the investor records the initial transaction, there is no need to adjust it, unless there is evidence that the fair market value of the investment has declined to below the recorded historical cost. If so, the investor writes down the recorded cost of the investment to its new fair market value.

If there is evidence that the fair market value has increased above the historical cost, it is not permissible to increase the recorded value of the investment. This is a highly conservative approach to recording investments.

In addition to the points just noted, the following accounting rules also apply to the cost method:

- If the venture makes a distribution, the investor records it as income; there is no impact on the investment account.
- If the venture makes a distribution to the investor that is greater than the investor's share of earnings, then the excess amount is used to reduce the carrying value of the investment.
- If the venture has undistributed earnings, they do not appear in any way in the records of the investor.

EXAMPLE

Chatterley Investments acquires a 2% interest in Elder Care Housing for $500,000. In the most recent reporting period, Elder Care recognizes $100,000 of net income and distributes $20,000 to investors. Under the requirements of the cost method, Chatterley records its initial investment of $500,000 and its 2% share of the distribution. Chatterley does not make any other entries.

Changing Methods

If the investor's level of control over a venture changes, it may be necessary to alter the method used to account for the investment. The alternatives are:

- *Change from cost method to equity method.* This implies an increased level of control by the investor. Retroactively adjust the investment account as though the equity method had been used since the initial investment date.
- *Change from equity method to cost method.* This implies a reduced level of control by the investor. The basis for the cost method becomes the balance in the investment account as of the last day when the equity method was used. The rules used for the cost method now apply.

Transactions with a Real Estate Venture

A real estate venture may enter into a number of transactions with its investors, most of which involve funding transactions. The following sub-sections deal with the accounting to be used whenever these activities arise.

Contributions

An investor may contribute assets or services to a real estate venture. If so, the accounting treatment by the investor of these contributions is as follows:

- *Cash.* When cash is paid into a venture, always record it at the amount of cash invested, with no exceptions.
- *Real estate.* When real estate is contributed to a venture, record it at the carrying amount of the real estate. The investor cannot recognize a profit on the real estate at this time, since it is simply being shifted into an entity that the investor partially or fully owns. However, if the investor contributes real estate and then withdraws cash from the venture with no commitment to reinvest the cash, this can be considered a sale of an interest in the venture. If the carrying amount exceeds the fair value of the property, then write down the amount of the investment to its fair value. Such an impairment may be indicated when an investor contributes property to a venture in exchange for an unusually small ownership percentage in the venture.
- *Services.* Services may be contributed to a venture, such as legal advice or construction labor. This investment is to be recorded at its cost.

Loans

An investor may lend money to a real estate project. If so, the investor normally would record interest income from the loaned funds, with a portion deferred based on the investor's percentage interest in the venture's profits and losses. However, the investor should defer the recognition of any interest income on these loans under the following circumstances:

- Collection of the loan amount or the related interest is in doubt; this may not be an issue if there is adequate collateral on the loan.
- The other investors are not expected to accept their shares of any losses; this can increase the lending investor's share of any interest expense.
- The venture capitalizes the interest as part of its construction activities; recognition is deferred until the interest is eventually charged to expense by the venture.

In cases where all investors are required to lend money to a venture in proportion to their equity interests in the venture, these loans are to be accounted for as capital contributions. When this happens and the venture pays interest on the loans, the investors treat them as dividends. Thus, if an investment is being accounted for using the equity method, the payments characterized as dividends are subtracted from the net investment in the venture.

Purchase of Real Estate from a Venture

There may be a situation in which an investor in a real estate partnership purchases real estate from that partnership. If so, the investor cannot record as income its share of the venture's profit on the sale transaction. Instead, the investor's share of this income is recorded by the investor as a reduction of the carrying amount of the real estate that it has just purchased from the venture. This reduction in the carrying amount is gradually recognized as income as the real estate is depreciated over time. Or, if the investor later sells the real estate to a third party, any residual reduction in the carrying amount can be recognized as income at that time.

EXAMPLE

Mr. Noble buys a building from Archaic Partners for $1,000,000. Archaic recognizes a $200,000 profit on the transaction. Mr. Noble is a 25% investor in Archaic, and so would normally recognize a $50,000 profit from the partnership. However, since he bought the building, he must instead record the building at a carrying amount of $950,000.

Mr. Noble will depreciate the cost of the building over 30 years. He can recognize the $50,000 at the same pace, which will amount to $1,666.67 of profit recognition in each of the next 30 years.

Sale of an Investment in a Real Estate Venture

When an investor sells an investment in a real estate venture, this is the same as selling an interest in the underlying real estate. The sale of real estate is discussed in the Real Estate Sales chapter.

Real Estate Syndication

Real estate syndication occurs when an entity (usually a partnership, joint venture, or trust) raises funds from investors with the intent of using the money to acquire interests in real estate. In exchange for their money, investors are given a financial interest in the investing entity. Syndication activities relate to efforts to create these investing entities.

Syndication Activities

A syndicator earns a commission from investors by organizing syndication entities. More specifically, syndicators earn their fees by participating in the following core activities:

- Create syndication entities
- Sell interests in these entities to investors
- Arrange for the entities to purchase real estate, which can occur in the following ways:
    - Acquire properties from third parties
    - Acquire properties or options to purchase properties from the syndicator
    - Acquire properties that are being flipped by the syndicator
- Supervise the development of acquired real estate
- Provide property management services for acquired real estate

A syndicator may also be involved in financing activities on behalf of these entities, such as acquiring debt for use in purchasing real estate.

Syndicator Risks and Rewards

Depending on the type of transaction, a syndicator may have partial ownership of the properties acquired by or sold to a syndication entity. If so, the syndicator may have a significant risk of ownership. This risk can arise under the following circumstances:

- *Down payments.* The entity only makes a minor down payment on acquired properties; if these properties are already owned by the syndicator, there is a risk of nonpayment by the entity. Similarly, the syndicator may be paid with subordinated notes, which may not be repaid if there are more senior creditors.
- *Future support.* The syndicator is obliged to continue supporting properties once they have been syndicated.

- *General partnership.* The syndicator is a general partner in a syndication partnership, which exposes the syndicator to all risks incurred by the business.

Offsetting these risks are a number of methods by which a syndicator can be compensated, which include the following:

- Receive a percentage of all funds raised from investors
- Receive a percentage ownership interest in a syndication entity
- Sell properties to the syndication entity for a profit
- Receive a percentage of the gain on future sales of properties by the syndication entity
- Receive a fee for subsequent property management services

Income Recognition by Syndicators

As just noted, a syndicator can derive income from numerous sources. How is this income to be recognized?

If a syndicator is paid a fee in exchange for services to be performed at some point in the future, it cannot recognize these fees as income until the related services have actually been performed. Until that time, the fee is considered to be a liability for the syndicator.

From the perspective of the syndication entity, the fees paid to a syndicator can vary, depending on the circumstances. The following points address unusually high or low payments:

- *Unusually high payments.* If an excessive amount has been paid, recognize in the accounting records a reasonable fee amount, and record the difference as an upward adjustment to the sales value of the real estate. This means that a smaller profit will be recognized when the real estate is eventually sold.
- *Unusually low payments.* If an unusually low amount has been paid, recognize in the accounting records a reasonable fee amount, and record the difference as a downward adjustment to the sales value of the real estate. This means that a larger profit will be recognized when the real estate is eventually sold.

There are guidelines for determining whether the amounts paid to syndicators are excessive or unusually low. A payment is considered reasonable if both of the following conditions are true:

- The fee is within a range of similar fees charged by independent brokers for similar transactions; and
- The fee is adequate for reimbursing the syndicator for amounts it paid to third parties associated with the transaction.

When determining whether a payment to a syndicator is reasonable, it is necessary to include in the payment not only all cash and notes paid, but also the value of any partnership interest paid to the syndicator.

To gather information about similar transactions, consult with independent brokers, review industry monitoring reports, and peruse the details of publicly-offered transactions.

A syndicator cannot recognize any fees from its syndication activities until the following two requirements have been completed:

- The earnings process for the syndicator is complete; and
- Collectability of the related funds is reasonably assured.

A syndicator may face exposure to future costs from its involvement with the properties held by a syndication entity, such as debt guarantees and obligations to invest in upgrades. If these future support costs are material, the syndicator is required to defer the recognition of income from syndication fees until the future costs can be reasonably estimated. Income is to be reduced by the amount of these estimated costs. If the potential future costs cannot be estimated, the amount of income that a syndicator can recognize is reduced by the maximum amount of cost exposure.

EXAMPLE

Mellow Associates is a real estate syndicator. Mellow forms a partnership, Butterfly Partners, which invests in real estate. The intent of this partnership is to acquire distressed single-family homes, rent them for a period of time, and resell them when demand eventually increases. The initial transactions engaged in by Butterfly are as follows:

- The limited partners invest $95,000 and the general partner contributes $5,000.
- Butterfly buys a property from the syndicator for $400,000. The payment is comprised of $10,000 cash and the assumption of a $390,000 nonrecourse mortgage.

At the time of the purchase, the rent payments from the property are sufficient to cover the ongoing mortgage payments. Mellow receives a syndication fee that is comprised of $10,000 cash and a five-year senior note for $25,000 at the market rate of interest.

Scenario 1 – No Ongoing Syndicator Obligation

There is no indication that the syndicator will be involved with the property in the future, so there does not appear to be any future risk of loss. This means that both parts of the syndication fee can be recognized immediately by the syndicator. The syndicator may need to evaluate the collectability of the $25,000 senior note, and possibly create a bad debt reserve against it.

Scenario 2 – Subordinated Note as Part of Payment to Syndicator

If the five-year senior note for $25,000 had instead been designated as a subordinated note, the syndicator would instead recognize a profit only when it receives cash payments on the note.

Acquisition, Development, and Construction Arrangements

A lender may participate in the expected residual profits or cash flows of a property transaction for which the lender is providing funding, either through profit sharing or above-market interest rates or fees. The following characteristics suggest the presence of such an arrangement where the lender takes on the role of an investor:

- *Delinquency.* The debt is structured to avoid foreclosure by not requiring payments until project completion.
- *Fees.* The lender pays for the commitment or origination fees by including them in the loan.
- *Funding.* The lender provides substantially all of the required funding.
- *Interest.* The lender rolls substantially all of the interest and fees during the loan term back into the loan balance.
- *Recourse.* The lender only has recourse to the acquisition, development, and construction project.
- *Repayment.* The lender will only be repaid if the property is sold, refinanced, or begins to generate enough cash flow to service the loan.

Conversely, there are situations where the lender has not taken on the role of an investor, and is merely financing property. The following characteristics suggest the presence of a simple lending arrangement:

- *Borrower investment.* The borrower has a substantial equity investment in the project that is not funded by the lender. The value of the borrower's efforts (sweat equity) in the property development is not to be considered when evaluating the borrower's investment.
- *Collateral.* The lender has recourse to significant other assets of the borrower besides the project, and which are not also pledged as collateral elsewhere, or the lender has an irrevocable letter of credit from a third party for a substantial amount of the loan.
- *Net cash flow.* There are sufficient noncancelable sale or lease contracts from third parties to provide the cash flow needed to service the debt.
- *Profit participation.* The profit participation of the lender is less than half of the expected residual profit.
- *Take-out commitment.* The lender has obtained a take-out commitment for the full amount of its lending arrangement from a third party.

The existence of a personal guarantee is not usually considered sufficient for classifying a lending arrangement as not being an investment. However, this may be the case if the guarantee covers a large part of the loan, the payment ability of the guarantor can be reliably measured (as represented by assets placed in escrow, an irrevocable letter of credit, or financial results), enforcing the guarantee is possible, and there is a demonstrated intent to enforce the guarantee.

When judging the financial statements of a guarantor, place particular emphasis on the presence of sufficient liquidity to fulfill the guarantee, and whether the guarantor has other contingent liabilities.

Also, the initial determination of investment or loan status for the lender may change over time, if the underlying terms of an arrangement are altered. Consequently, reassess the accounting treatment whenever loan terms are altered. The following situations that alter a lending scenario can impact how a lending arrangement is classified:

- *Risk reduction.* If the lender's risk diminishes significantly, an initial classification as an investment or joint venture might be reclassified as a loan.
- *Risk increase.* If the lender's risk increases (such as by releasing collateral) or the lender assumes a greater percentage of expected profits, an initial classification as a loan might be reclassified as an investment.

The initial accounting by a lender in an acquisition, development, and construction project is to be accounted for in one of two ways:

- *As an investment.* If the lender expects to receive more than 50% of the expected residual profit from a project, any income or loss from the arrangement is to be accounted for by the lender as a real estate investment.
- *As a loan.* If the lender expects to receive 50% or less of the expected residual profit from a project and there is a qualifying personal guarantee (as just described), the arrangement is to be accounted for as a loan. If the guarantee is not present, account for the arrangement as a real estate joint venture.

If a lender were to subsequently sell its share of any expected residual profits, there are two ways to account for the sale:

- *As an investment.* If the arrangement has been accounted for as an investment, the lender can account for the sale as a gain.
- *As a loan.* If the arrangement has been accounted for as a loan, the lender should recognize the proceeds from the sale as additional interest over the remaining term of the loan.

Participating Mortgage Loans

A participating mortgage loan is one in which the lender can participate in the results of operations of the real estate operation being mortgaged, or in any appreciation in the market value of the real estate.

The borrower should account for a participating mortgage loan by recognizing a participation liability that is based on the fair value of the participation feature at the start of the loan. The offset to this liability is the debt discount account. Subsequently, the borrower accounts for the following issues related to the participating mortgage loan:

- *Interest.* Charge to expense any periodic interest expense amounts so designated in the mortgage agreement.
- *Amortization.* Amortize the amount of the debt discount related to the lender's participation in the profits of the real estate venture, using the interest method.
- *Participation payments.* Pay the lender for its share of profits of the real estate venture, and charge this amount to interest expense. The offset is to the participation liability account.
- *Participation adjustment.* At the end of each reporting period, adjust the participation liability to match the latest fair value of the participation feature.

If the mortgage loan is extinguished prior to its due date, recognize a debt extinguishment gain or loss on the difference between the recorded amount of the debt and the amount paid or exchanged to settle the debt liability.

EXAMPLE

Domicilio Corporation develops residential real estate in the Miami area. On April 1, 20X1, Domicilio buys a property for $20,000,000. Domicilio obtains the funding for this purchase primarily with a $15 million participating mortgage loan from Primero Bank. The loan agreement is for four years, and requires interest-only payments at a 6% interest rate, until a balloon payment is required at the end of the loan term. In addition, Primero will receive a 10% participation in the profits from the sale of each residential unit, payable at the maturity of the loan.

The initial estimate of the fair value of the participation feature is $60,000, so Domicilio records the following initial entry for the loan:

	Debit	Credit
Cash	15,000,000	
Loan discount	60,000	
Mortgage loan payable		15,000,000
Participation liability		60,000

At the end of one year, Domicilio records the following entry related to the interest expense paid on the mortgage, and the amortization of the discount on the mortgage (using straight-line amortization):

	Debit	Credit
Interest expense	915,000	
Cash		900,000
Loan discount		15,000

Midway through the next year, Domicilio adjusts its estimate of the fair value of the participation feature upward by $22,000. This results in the following entry:

	Debit	Credit
Loan discount	22,000	
Participation liability		22,000

Thus, 18 months into the participating mortgage loan, the participation liability recorded by Domicilio has increased to $82,000, while the balance in the loan discount account has increased to $67,000.

Real Estate Investment Trusts

A real estate investment trust (REIT) is an entity that employs capital and debt to make investments and loans related to real estate. If an REIT elects a certain tax status, it can avoid paying federal income taxes by distributing at least 90% of its taxable income to its shareholders.

An REIT may create a service corporation, which is an entity that performs services for the trust or other entities, such as property management, construction, financing, and sales. An REIT is considered to have significant influence over a service corporation when some or all of the following conditions are present:

- The service corporation's activities primarily support the REIT
- Substantially all of the economic benefits derived by the service corporation flow to the REIT
- The REIT can designate a position on the board of the service corporation
- Both entities share board members
- Both entities share officers and/or employees
- The majority voting owners of the service corporation have not contributed substantial equity to the corporation
- The REIT's managers influence the operational decisions of the service corporation
- The REIT can obtain the service corporation's financial statements in order to track its investment in the corporation using the equity method

If significant influence is present, the REIT should account for its investment in the service corporation using the equity method, not the cost method.

An REIT may issue loans as part of its business operations. The REIT should stop recognizing interest revenue on these loans when it cannot reasonably expect to receive the revenue. The following conditions can indicate that such recognition should be terminated:

- Payments are past due on the principal or interest
- The borrower has defaulted on the terms of the loan

- The creditworthiness of the borrower is in doubt
- The loan has already been renegotiated
- The REIT expects to initiate foreclosure proceedings, or has already done so
- There are construction delays or cost overruns that impede the viability of the project

Presentation and Disclosure Topics

An investor in a real estate venture can, under certain circumstances, continue to record its share of losses in the venture using the equity method, even though its investment has been wiped out. When this excess loss is recorded, it must be presented as a liability in the investor's financial statements.

When an investor uses the equity method to account for an investment, it should state the investment as a single line item in the balance sheet. Similarly, the investor should report its share of any venture gains or losses as a single line item in the income statement.

An entity may do business with a variety of parties with which it has a close association. These parties are known as related parties, of which examples are:

- Affiliates
- Other subsidiaries under common control
- Owners of a business, its managers, and their families
- The parent entity

There are many types of transactions that can be conducted between related parties, such as sales, asset transfers, leases, lending arrangements, guarantees, allocations of common costs, and the filing of consolidated tax returns. Many of these arrangements may exist between a real estate venture and its investors.

The disclosure of related party information is considered useful to the readers of a company's financial statements, particularly in regard to the examination of changes in the financial results and financial position over time, and in comparison to the same information for other businesses.

In general, any related party transaction should be disclosed that would impact the decision making of the users of a company's financial statements. This involves the following disclosures:

- *General*. Disclose all material related party transactions, including the nature of the relationship, the nature of the transactions, the dollar amounts of the transactions, the amounts due to or from related parties and the settlement terms (including tax-related balances), and the method by which any current and deferred tax expense is allocated to the members of a group. Do not include compensation arrangements, expense allowances, or any transactions that are eliminated in the consolidation of financial statements.
- *Control relationship*. Disclose the nature of any control relationship where the organization and other entities are under common ownership or management control, and this control could yield results different from what would

be the case if the other entities were not under similar control, even if there are no transactions between the businesses.

- *Receivables*. Separately disclose any receivables from officers, employees, or affiliated entities.

Depending on the transactions, it may be acceptable to aggregate some related party information by type of transaction. Also, it may be necessary to disclose the name of a related party, if doing so is required to understand the relationship.

When disclosing related party information, do not state or imply that the transactions were on an arm's-length basis, unless the claim can be substantiated.

Summary

An investor in a real estate venture needs a high level of accounting expertise in order to produce investment records that faithfully reflect the relationship. This is most likely to involve the use of the equity method of accounting, along with continuing adjustments to the investment amount that are required under that method. The investment method may also change, depending on the level of investment in and control over a venture. Further, the investor may engage in any number of operational or financing arrangements with a venture, which may require the deferral of related profits. In short, the accounting for real estate ventures can require a considerable amount of detailed attention.

Chapter 11
Housing Associations

Introduction

This chapter contains descriptions of several housing associations that may be created as part of a real estate development, special accounting rules to which they are subjected, and the types of disclosures that they are required to make in their financial statements.

Common Interest Realty Associations

A common interest realty association is an association of owners that is responsible for the provision of services and the maintenance of property that is shared by or owned in common by the owners. Examples of this type of association are:

- Condominium associations
- Cooperative housing corporation (a coop)
- Homeowners' associations
- Time-share associations

This type of ownership situation typically has the following characteristics:

- Owners own specific lots or interior spaces, or own shares of stock in a property
- Owners have an undivided interest in common property
- Owners are automatically assigned ownership in an association that maintains property and provides services
- Owners are assessed an amount at intervals to fund the association

An association should recognize revenue as deferred revenue when it is a special assessment designed to pay for specific costs that have not yet been incurred. These amounts should only be reported as revenue when there are offsetting expenses. All other special assessments can be recognized as revenue in the periods in which they are assessed, irrespective of whether they have been collected.

If an association uses fund accounting, it should charge expenditures for major repairs and replacements to the fund established for that purpose. If such an expenditure relates to common property, report the expenditure as a transfer from the major repairs and replacements fund to the operating fund.

A common interest realty association (other than a coop, as discussed in the following section) recognizes non-unit real property as an asset, but only when it has title or other evidence of ownership, and when either of the following conditions is present:

- The association can dispose of the property and retain the proceeds; or
- The property is used by the association to produce significant cash flows based on usage

These assets are to be recognized at their acquisition cost. If an asset was acquired through a non-monetary transaction, such as a transfer from a developer, the association should recognize the asset at its fair value on the acquisition date. In the latter case, it can be useful to consider the developer's cost when deriving the fair value figure. Once recognized, these assets shall be depreciated over their useful lives.

All types of common interest realty associations should recognize common personal property as assets. Examples of these assets are furnishings, recreation equipment, and vehicles that are employed to operate, maintain, or replace common property.

When a common interest realty association receives assets from a developer and recognizes them in its balance sheet, the assets should be reported as additions to the balance of the association's operating fund. If the association does not issue assessments to its members for future major repairs and replacements to property, it may not be necessary to use fund reporting.

Issues Specific to Cooperative Housing Associations

A cooperative should recognize common real property as an asset of the association. This is because the legal structure of this entity gives it title to all common property, and allows it to dispose of these assets. This is not the case for most other types of common interest realty associations.

Presentation and Disclosure Topics

This section contains the decidedly voluminous financial statement presentation and disclosure requirements for housing associations, with separate treatment of common interest realty associations and cooperative housing associations.

Common Interest Realty Association Presentation Requirements

A full set of financial statements for a common interest realty association should include the following:

- Balance sheet
- Statement of revenues and expenses
- Statement of changes in fund balances or statement of changes in members' equity
- Statement of cash flows
- Accompanying notes to the financial statements

The statement of revenues and expenses should present information about an association's assessments, other revenues, and operational expenses. All activities other than the major repairs and replacement fund should be reported in this statement.

Depreciation expense is reported within the fund in which the related asset is reported.

The statement of changes in fund balances reconciles the beginning and ending balance in each fund. Reconciling items relate to the activities occurring within each reporting period including inter-fund receivables and payables. If there is a transfer between funds, this is presented as an inter-fund transfer, and not as revenue to the receiving fund.

EXAMPLE

The directors of the Willow Creek Association note that there are $50,000 of excess operating funds as of the end of the last year of operations, and decide to transfer it to the association's major repairs and replacements fund. In the statement of changes for the replacement fund, the incoming funds appear as a transfer, not as revenue.

Reported revenue should be broken down into categories to clarify sources, such as:

- Assessments charged to the developer
- Developer contributions and subsidies
- Interest income
- Lawsuit settlements
- Special-use charges
- Vending income

These classifications can be combined if they are not material. Interest income should be associated with a specific fund, unless the association has a policy for presenting it in a different manner.

When a common interest realty association issues periodic assessments to owners for future major repairs and replacements, it must present these amounts separately in its balance sheet from the amounts it assesses owners for normal operations. If fund reporting is used, these major assessments are to be reported in a fund that is separate from the operating fund. If an association also conducts commercial operations, these activities can be reported in separate funds.

When an association reports about an operating fund, it should provide several types of information to give the reader a full understanding of the status of the fund. This information should include the cash balance, assessments receivable, prepaid expenses, and accounts payable, as well as any property and equipment that have been reported as assets.

When an association reports about a major repairs and replacements fund, it should provide detailed information about all assets held for future replacement funding, such as cash, marketable securities, and short-term investments, as well as liabilities.

Common Interest Realty Association Disclosures

When a common interest realty association releases its financial statements, they should be accompanied by the following disclosures:

- The legal form of the entity (usually a corporation or association)
- The legal form of the entity for which the association provides services (such as a condominium or cooperative)
- The areas controlled by the association and the number of units (a coop may instead disclose the number of shares, while a time-share association may disclose the number of weeks)
- The services provided by the association (such as facility maintenance)
- Any subsidies provided by the developer
- The number of units, coop shares, or time-share weeks owned by the developer
- The proposed use of funds collected via special assessments
- The purposes to which assessments were put when the use differed from their original designation
- The funding for future major repairs and replacements, which includes the following information:

  - Any requirements to accumulate funds, and the association's compliance with those requirements
  - The association's funding policy (if any), and its compliance with that policy
  - The amounts assessed in the current period for major repairs and replacements
  - If a special assessment or borrowing was used to fund future major repairs and replacements, disclose this information
  - A statement that funds are being accumulated based on current or projected costs, that actual expenditures may vary from these estimates, and that there may be material variances from expectations
  - A statement noting whether a study was completed to estimate the remaining useful lives of common property and the costs of future major repairs and replacements

- The association's income tax filing status and income tax liability
- Any credits from taxation authorities that will be phased out in future periods

An association should also disclose the following unaudited information:

- Estimates of current or future major repairs and replacements, including the following information:
    o The methods used to determine costs
    o The basis for calculations (such as the interest rates and inflation rates used)
    o The sources used
    o The dates of the studies conducted

- The components to be repaired or replaced, their estimated remaining useful lives and replacement costs, and the funds accumulated for each one

The following information should be disclosed about common property:

- The association's policy for recognizing and measuring common property
- A description of the common property recognized by the association in its balance sheet
- A description of any common property not recognized by the association in its balance sheet, but to which it has title or other evidence of ownership
- A statement regarding the association's responsibility to preserve and maintain the common property
- The terms and conditions associated with existing leases
- Any restrictions on the use of common property, or on how it can be dispositioned
- The depreciation expense for the reporting period
- The ending balances and accumulated depreciation in the major classes of depreciable assets
- A description of the methods used to calculate depreciation for the major classes of depreciable assets

Further, an association should disclose the proposed use of funds that have been collected through special assessments, as well as assessments used for alternative purposes than their original designations.

If at least 10% of the revenues of an association are derived from any one source (such as a developer or other third party), disclose the amount of revenue from each source.

It is possible that related parties are providing an association with insurance, maintenance assistance, or management services. In general, any related party transaction should be disclosed that would impact the decision making of the users of an association's financial statements. This involves the following disclosures:

- *General.* Disclose all material related party transactions, including the nature of the relationship, the nature of the transactions, the dollar amounts of the transactions, the amounts due to or from related parties and the settlement terms.

- *Control relationship.* Disclose the nature of any control relationship where the association and other entities are under common ownership or management control, and this control could yield results different from what would be the case if the other entities were not under similar control, even if there are no transactions between the businesses.
- *Receivables.* Separately disclose any receivables from officers, employees, or affiliated entities.

Depending on the transactions, it may be acceptable to aggregate some related party information by type of transaction. Also, it may be necessary to disclose the name of a related party, if doing so is required to understand the relationship.

When disclosing related party information, do not state or imply that the transactions were on an arm's-length basis, unless the claim can be substantiated.

Cooperative Housing Association Presentation Requirements

A full set of financial statements for a cooperative housing association is somewhat different from the requirement for the basic common interest realty association. The statements for a cooperative entity should include the following:

- Balance sheet
- Statement of operations
- Statement of changes in shareholders' equity
- Statement of cash flows
- Accompanying notes to the financial statements

The reported revenues for a cooperative should inform the reader about all charges to tenants and other income. If there is activity in the paid-in capital account, a cooperative should also prepare a statement of shareholders' equity.

Cooperative Housing Corporation Disclosures

A cooperative should include in its disclosures a discussion of its funding policy (if any) for future major repairs and replacements.

A cooperative should not disclose the components of its retained earnings, nor should it allocate a portion of its retained earnings to an amount equal to accumulated depreciation.

Summary

There is a major emphasis in this chapter on the reporting requirements of housing associations. In general, the accountant should assume that more disclosure of information is better than less, since the financial statements of these entities may be perused by contributing property owners, who want to know how their assessments are being used.

Glossary

A

Accretion expense. An expense arising from an increase in the carrying amount of the liability associated with an asset retirement obligation.

Accrual basis of accounting. A system for recording revenues when earned and expenses as incurred.

Acquisition, development, and construction arrangement. An arrangement where a lender participates in the expected residual profits resulting from the sale of real estate.

Amenities. Any features that improve the perceived attractiveness of a property, such as a swimming pool or a club house.

Asset retirement obligation. A liability associated with the retirement of a fixed asset.

Association. An organization of owners that manages common property.

Assumption. When one debtor takes over a debt from another party.

B

Blind pool. A partnership in which investment units are being or have been sold before the properties to be acquired have been specifically identified.

C

Cash basis of accounting. A system for recording revenues when cash is received and expenses when cash is paid out.

Common costs. Costs relating to at least two units or phases in a time-sharing or real estate project.

Common interest realty association. An association that governs and is funded by a common interest community.

Common property. Property for which title is held either by individual members in common, or by a common interest realty association.

Condominium. Property that combines exclusive ownership of a specific space with an undivided interest in common property.

Continuing investments. The aggregate of a buyer's payments to date for the purchase of a time-sharing interval, not including interest payments.

Continuing involvement. When the seller has not transferred substantially all of the benefits and risks related to real estate ownership to a third party.

Contract-for-deed. A contract in which the seller agrees to transfer title to the buyer, once a certain portion of the total price has been paid.

Cooperative housing corporation. An entity that owns real estate and is responsible for its maintenance and debt payments. Tenants own shares in the entity. Also known as a coop.

Corporate joint venture. A corporation that is owned by a group of joint venturers, for their benefit.

Cost recovery method. An income recognition method that delays profit recognition until the cash payments received exceed the cost of the property sold.

D

Deposit method. A method of accounting for a time-share sale, where cash received from a buyer is recorded as a deposit and a liability.

Downgrade. When the holder of a time-sharing interval exchanges it with the seller for a lower-value time interval; this exchange takes place because the holder may be unable to fulfill its payment obligations for the original interval.

F

Fair value. The price that would be received when an asset is sold in an orderly transaction between market participants.

Fixed time. A time-share arrangement in which the buyer purchases a specific period.

Flip transaction. When a syndicator acquires an ownership interest and resells it to a syndication entity, such as a partnership.

Floating time. A time-share arrangement in which the buyer is not restricted to a specific time period.

Fractional interest. The ownership of a partial interest in real estate that typically involves larger blocks of usage time.

Full accrual method. A profit recognition method where the profit associated with a transaction is recognized in full.

G

GAAP. The acronym for Generally Accepted Accounting Principles, which is one of the major accounting frameworks.

General ledger. The master set of accounts that summarize all transactions occurring within an entity.

General partnership. An entity in which each partner has unlimited liability.

H

Holding period. The time interval during which a time-sharing interval is held for sale.

I

Incentive. Something offered by the seller of a time-sharing interval to a buyer for less than its fair value, usually provided at the point of sale.

Incidental operations. Activities that generate revenue during the period when a property is being developed or held, with the intent of reducing the development cost.

Indirect project costs. Costs incurred after a property has been obtained, and which clearly relate to projects under development.

Inducement. Something offered by the seller of a time-sharing interval to a buyer for less than its fair value, even if a time-sharing sale does not occur.

Installment method. A method for apportioning cash receipts from a buyer between costs recovered and profits.

Integral equipment. A structure or equipment that cannot be removed from real estate without incurring a significant cost.

Interval. A specific period of time during which a time-sharing unit is apportioned to a customer.

J

Joint control. A situation in which the operational or financing decisions needed to operate a business require the approval of at least two of its owners.

L

Limited partnership. An entity in which there is at least one general partner and at least one limited partner.

M

Mini-vacation. A marketing program under which a time-share seller offers the subsidized short-term use of a time-share unit to a customer in exchange for attending a sales presentation.

N

Noncontrolling interest. That portion of the net assets of a subsidiary not attributable to a parent.

Nonreciprocal transfer. A transfer of assets or services in one direction.

O

Orphan share. The share of liability for environmental remediation costs attributable to other parties that exceeds the amount for which those parties have already settled their liability.

Owners association. A group of owners that administers the rules and regulations of a time-sharing project.

Ownership interest. The title to real estate, or an option to acquire real estate.

P

Percentage-of-completion method. A method for determining the profit to be recognized for a time-sharing transaction, where revenue recognition at the sale date is based on the proportion of costs incurred-to-date to the combination of costs incurred-to-date and costs still to be incurred.

Phase. A distinguishable portion of a real estate or time-sharing project.

Planned amenities. Amenities that are to be constructed, but for which there is no construction obligation under the agreements with time-share purchasers.

Points. Purchased vacation credits that can be used to occupy units at different locations.

Preacquisition costs. Costs related to the acquisition of a property, but before the property has been legally acquired, such as surveying and zoning costs.

Project costs. Those costs directly related to the acquisition and construction of a real estate project.

Promised amenities. Amenities that a developer is required to complete under the agreements with time-share purchasers.

R

Real estate investment trust. An entity that employs capital and debt to make investments and loans related to real estate, and which must distribute substantially all of its taxable income to its shareholders each year.

Real property. Any property attached to land, as well as the land itself.

Recourse. The right of the recipient of receivables to be paid by the transferring entity when debtors do not pay.

Reduced-profit method. The calculation of profit by discounting a receivable to the present value of the lowest level of allowed payments over the maximum payment period.

Relative sales value method. A method used to allocate inventory costs and to derive the cost of sales related to a sale. The cost of sales is calculated as a percentage of net sales and the estimated cost-of-sales percentage.

Reload. When a customer is given a second time-sharing interval while retaining the right to the first interval.

Reload interval. The sale of a new time-sharing interval that is treated as a separate transaction.

Rescission. The right of a buyer to cancel an existing sales contract within a certain period of time and be paid back by the seller.

Right-to-use. A time-sharing sale under which ownership of the real estate is retained by the seller.

S

Sales value. A derivation of the amount at which a time-sharing interval would sell in an all-cash transaction.

Sampler program. A marketing program under which a time-share seller offers a reduced-rate stay to a customer who has previously toured a developer project, in exchange for taking a subsequent tour of the project. The customer's reduced-rate charge might be applied against the price of a time-share sale.

Seller subsidy. An amount paid by the seller of time-share intervals to an owners' association to offset any losses incurred by the association.

Service corporation. An entity created by a real estate investment trust to perform services for the trust or other entities.

Syndication activities. Those efforts involved in forming an entity that acquires real estate after raising funds from investors.

Syndication fees. Any compensation paid to a syndicator for selling interests in a syndication entity, such as a partnership.

T

Tenancy-for-years. A time-sharing arrangement in which a customer can use a time-sharing interval for a specific number of years.

Time-sharing. The conveyance of a right to occupy a dwelling unit during specific future periods.

U

Uncollectability. When the seller of a time-sharing interval is unable to collect all amounts due.

Undivided interest. An arrangement where there is joint ownership of property, and where each of the owners has an unrestricted claim to the property, but where no owner has an exclusive claim to any property.

Unit. The space in a time-sharing project that is to be occupied by a customer.

Upgrade. A transaction in which a time-share customer transfers from ownership of a lower-priced to a higher-priced time-sharing interval.

V

Vacation club. A time-sharing arrangement that gives a buyer the right to use units at all resorts owned by the club, along with other benefits.

Index

Made in the USA
Monee, IL
27 April 2021

67005571R00116